MY BOOK OF
COLORS

MARSHALL ELMORE

SWEETSPIRE LITERATURE
——— MANAGEMENT ———

CONTENTS

A New Chapter

So, this is it
I say welcome
To a new chapter of my ever-changing life
I will make mistakes

The path will be long
I will live and learn
I will welcome every day
Touch every soul

Tell the ones who care enough
I finally made it
Out of the cold
Look at my face

All the tells I will tell I cannot erase
On this long road, I take
With the stories I make
Just a little something to remind you of me

I am here
On the road to happiness
And along the way
Is paved with good intentions

Love, compassion, and good deeds
So, this is it
I say welcome
To a new chapter of my ever-changing life

March 29, 2022

A Place to Be Free

As the light turns to darkness
I wander aimlessly about with fear
Empty smiles
Hiding hollowness within

Ten thousand thoughts
As I look out my window
I cover my eyes as if to hide
To erase the promises, I made

I want to be a better man
Strength pushes me to start again
I will walk the path
Somewhere out there

Is a place of peace
Calling out and beckoning
To be a better man
Except the life to make

But were the choice presented
The walls I built around the truth
I closely guard within
No matter where it leads

Put aside my burdens
Put away my fears
Until the very end
It is calling to me

Beckoning me
So, I will uncover my eyes
And fill my soul within
There is a place where I can be free

May 9, 2022

About It

Another is what you wanted
While the world was in the palm of your hand
Could have given you all but you wanted another
Just like your love

Along with the answer why
Breaking the unconditional bond
Or until the end
How could I have been so wrong?

So, I stop the worries
And thoughts overall
Till I am sick and unhappy about it
How could it just end this way?

Left with my confusion about it
Only to feel down and blue about it
How could you leave me this way?
Now I think about how unfair about it

Is it really going down this way?
All I can remember is you saying goodbye
I should know better to answer your calls
Let know I was crying on the other line

Watch you breaking hearts
Was I living a lie?
In time you will realize
I was the best you had about it

January 11, 2022

All In My Dreams

Believer of imagination
Limiting causation
Hearing thunder tumble
Mountain's crumble

Church bells ring
Lion tamers sing
A love story will unfold
A ravens call bold

Family and friends
That never ends
All in my dreams
Crossing streams

Beauty all around
In and out of town
Even build a wall around
Multitude still found

January 18, 2022

Almost Heaven

I saw my angel on the windowsill
Pointing to the exit sign
As I walked in my frozen steps
To a summer's crossing

Into a heavens gate
Where choir singing echoed
And songbirds sung
So, too could candles burn bright

At night side by side
Forever reaching to light
It is almost heaven
But it is my own reflection

February 12, 2022

Always Remember

Things in life take time
Other people are not happy or rhyme

Grow and never stop working on yourself
The change will happen do not stay on a bookshelf

Mistakes do not define you
You are powerful and capable of all you do

January 22, 2022

Ameliorating

There is a strong awakening
In feeling, you deserve more
Or the desire for a better you
In that is the realization of potential

To no longer settle
Or avoid possibilities
Ameliorating is now all you know
With patients and acceptance

Being yourself will come easily

January 3, 2022

Anathema of My Soul

Could I be content
In a world, I hold in this heart
Brought me to sunny days
Stare at my perfect future

I will stand tall
Shut my mouth to what I hate
I will be who I am again
My words will cut like swords

Impress on everyone
The anathema of my soul
No one will lose me
I am tied to this world

Happiness in fallen tears
I know where this will take me
Facing gratefulness deep inside
Gaining control of all I know

May 9, 2022

Angels Need Me

The sun never came up
Yet it seems to be all around
I am a believer
Because I see it completely now

It is my time to let go
How tears may shed
But angels need me now
Angels need me to come home to you

As I take a hand
Stay strong and surrender
I lived a happy life
With love in my heart

I need to let go now
Do not cry just dry your eyes
The angels need me now
Calling me home to see you

February 27, 2022

Answer the Phone

Cannot answer the phone
Just need a moment
Do not take it personal
Room is dark

No reason to see me cry
I know you understand
But why?
Because when I am done

I must be Superman
My misery will be my server
I cannot be my best right now
So, fire away at me

With your words
I am more awake now than ever
I will be alright
There is another day

Fire burns in my eyes
I will keep me safe
I will be on my way
But I cannot answer the phone

February 28, 2022

Anxiety

Anxiety as you watch over me
To be the one to be
Listening to the news
Thinking of the blues

In a world of cruel
Horrible, unjust, and drool
But I flip my mind to
Things that matter most to me and true

Like warming my feet under my dog
And being next to someone's heartbeat like a log
Or someone hearing mine
Smelling fresh cut grass while driving so fine

Crying to a beautiful song
And being kissed by a loved one all day long
Buying something cheaper than the tag says
And walking by the mirror and doing a double-take gee wiz

Saying I love you to people on the phone
And wishing people well that hurt me that I have known
I love that I cry in the presence of the lord
Yes, it is these little things that bring me the peace I look toward

March 22, 2022

Appreciate It

Start to live in a moment
Live the best in all moments
The ego will know
Nothing will go wrong

And nothing ruined at all
Condition the soul
It is not hard it has been told
With experience in life

Dreams and feelings will start
Ego is afraid it will stop
Life is not about the next next
It is about the here and now

Uncertainty and the presence
Making life possible
Appreciating everything now
No worries about future

Be mindfulness
Counting your blessings
Channeling energy
Appreciating your life

Letting positive energy occupy space
No room for negative energy
Do not fear life
Appreciate it

January 8, 2022

Are You Here

If I am right
Slowly losing my mind
Would I be fine?
Could I be wrong

Could I be right
Would the stars align just, right?
But it is just fine
I have been wasting my time

Do not mind
I am still breathing air
Being half alive
Overlook my mind

At least you are here
Would it be fine?
If I am right
Or am I wrong

May 6, 2022

Ask the Bartender

One drink makes you happy
And another one makes you feel good
And the one that the bartender gives you
Seems stronger because it is free

Go ask the bartender
When she is being generous
And if you go chasing the sobriety chip
And you know you are going to fall

Tell your sponsor
Give him a call
Go to the bar
When you are feeling small

When your friends come around
They tell you where to go
And your wagon just tipped over
And your mind is moving slow

Go ask the bartender
I think she will know
How to scratch your itch
Now everyone is talking backward

March 30, 2022

Baby Love Lady Bug

The power in my body
Like tides in the ocean
An intoxicating ride
A current you cannot deny

My blessings grow heavy
Pulling all to the abyss
I sense the tremor of the deep
I know that I must leave

Leaving love in my wake
Surges all that I can be
While destroying dread
And uprooting time

I will keep these memories
As the ocean swells
Like the tides intoxicate me
My body clams this power

March 28, 2022

Backward Will

There has been so much time lost
In this backward will
Across open oceans
That poisoned me

Collecting people
Along the way
So, I am on the move
Searching for you

Yet again on that open ocean
I cannot lie
How I feel
I am but a mess of bones

And I feel like a mess of skin
I need to be saved from
The hell I am in
Because I am in a fantasy

Every time I think of you
I see the dark, I hear the howling winds
There has been so much time lost
In this backward will

May 11, 2022

Be Here

Will you lead to your ways?
And then leave me right there
In my innocence
Like a prize, I won

Or a smile I earned
No more a slave to me
Or the words you prove
I live beneath the truth

Feeling the skin deep too
I will always be here
Hanging on the world
Feeling with your skin

Will, I always be here
Your burning eyes
Cause flames to arise
Or will I always be here

January 27, 2022

Be Vulnerable

Do not let love pass you by
When you want it bad
It is in your blood
Be vulnerable and go for it

It may surprise you what could be
The very heart of you
Makes you want to breathe
You will not leave

You will love
But you tell it now
And show it
Show the moon above

Always by your side
Only think of you
Love has been our destiny
Since the beginning of time

So, start with a kiss to prove it
Swallow any foolish pride
When you want it bad
Do not let love pass you by

April 3, 2022

Beats the Blood

Into my arms, you will be
As I lay your body down
To a trembling heart
That shivers with the cold

How it beats the blood for you
Can you not hear the sound?
For it is the beat of a hundred drums
Playing your song

I carry the rarest of roses
In the palm of my hand
Winter in its cruel ways
Took others way too soon

In the loneliness and hopelessness
Only to scratch what is left of the time
And what is left of the world
There is no greater love than mine

I will be the only one
To keep you from the cold
Winters chill to heaven's gate
With stars of brightest gold

They shine for you
Burning at both ends
Come into these arms again
And set this spirit free

March 22, 2022

Believe in Strength

We get chances
We have choices
We have opportunities
We make decisions

Surround yourself
With people
That are dreamers
That are thinkers

People that want to do
And ones that want
Want to believe
In themselves

But most of all
Surround yourself with people
That know your greatness
Ones that believe in you

There will be days
You will need this strength
When you do not believe
In yourself

March 14, 2022

Better Choices

You lie waste with the demons
There is no place for you here
You pick and choose your position
So, you can be homeless

Because your actions are a message
Send my regards to hell
Fall upon your knees
One, two, three

This is your soul
You can beg and plead
You have power and control
Do not push the blame on me

This is for your soul to bare
You have been given a life to live
Say goodbye to your faith
And your promises too

But your heart is racing
You want something better
As it beats out your mouth
This is your body and soul

May 11, 2022

Black Soul Upon Me

Lights black sublimity
Of the night's sun
Keeper of the wild
And the beating of the stars

Charmer of souls
And a master of death
Savage of night
Sheathe upon me

Oh, dark bright one
Intertwine my being with you
Explore my spirit with deep voyages of joy
Take residence in me

Giver of torture and elation
Touch my flesh with your black masses
Outré night
Unbound me

April 26, 2022

Brave Enough

I would save you from the sea
And pull you from the flames that be
Take away the shadows that leave you standing
Alone in open skies

It is in my devotion that I give you
Until the end of time
So, you will not be forgotten
Because it is I that will be by your side

Take my life
So, you can live
My life is nothing if yours is out
I have no reason but to die

But if I am standing with my emotions in my hands
Looking to the brightest star in the sky
Because no matter where my thoughts take me
In death, I will survive

And I will never be forgotten
With you by my side
And I will let the devil know
That I was brave enough to die

March 23, 2022

Break the Dam

Wisdom is given freely
Patience is used wisely
But falling in love with you
Is the right thing to do

I will right all the wrongs
Break the dams that stop the flow
This sea of love
Is ours to hold

So, take my hand
This is meant to be
Like falling in love
You and me

March 2, 2022

Breaking the Rules

Getting older is not for wimps
I cannot hear, smell, or see
Looking for love
But it is right around the corner

I run through streetlights
I am taking chances
Breaking the rules
Nobody can tell me what to do

Making my own way
Being someone, I can be proud of
Till the end
Getting older is not for wimps

February 27, 2022

Breathe Down My Neck

Lucid
But dreaming
Created a city to roam
And a pond with no borders

Only to watch you drown
I am petrified
To a warm wind on the back of my neck
A breath breathing

If only I could move
I would not lose you
So, I sleep all-day
Lucid

But it is a dream
No face but it is you
Keeping me half awake
I will sleep

So, I can keep you here with me
Eyes closed almost there
Back home to the moon
Only to hit the rewind

Falling into darkness
The pond is pitiless
Why do I?
Sleep at all

In the haunt, I created in my mind
Lucid
But I am dreaming
A face always askew

But I am never fully asleep
And I want to sleep
I want to keep you here with me
It is not fair to be without you

April 27, 2022

Breathe Into Me

I have an invitation to death
Come into my easeful future
Death how I long for thee
Nurture

Will you nurture me into the afterlife?
Breathe
Breathe into me
Companion

Death my only companion
I was born of this pain
And it will not go away
Take this life as a gift

And put it on thy self
A soul full of pain
My body is modest to hold so much
So, breathe into me

March 27, 2022

Bright Side of This Morning

I had a dream
We were together on a day of fun
Driving my truck, you were the highest
I could not get enough

Somewhere in the day
We saw eye to eye
Magic and sparks flowing
Now you could not get enough

All we want to know
Where is this going now
Do not want to go home
Stay right here is my new home

Who would I be if I walked away?
Through the bright side of a morning
Or the rock that rolled this feeling
The sun will not let me sleep

Or walk back to the truck
I am too drunk on you
And I cannot be alone
Going through the bright side of this morning

February 19, 2022

Bring Back the Night

The night takes over a dying sun
To watch the ascent and fall
The power struggle begins in a faded glow
Cover us

Protect us
Take the night into the fire
It leads us to fall
Walkthrough imitations of hell

Listen to the rhythm of the beat
The drums from afar
The guilty with sin
Hanging from the trees

Cries from the deep
Forgotten and abandoned
Pleading unheeded
The millions of unknown

Walk till the sun will rise
The nonstop a million calls
I know your name
I have defeated you before

I know what demons kill me
And visions of hell
Submit to temptation taunting my soul
Unlock these restraints

Cover us all
Help us till the sun meets us all
Endure and persist
No mercy without

Time is on our side
Safe and unaware
With a million dreams
Love unites

Love unites us all
The power to conquer here in our hearts
Eternal as time
Love will conquer all

May 8, 2022

Brother

Oh, brother my brother
I was a king
You were the knight
Young in are ways

We took the night
Ruled the days
Hung on every word
Dug trenches

And made our forts
If I was dying on my knees
You would be the one to rescue me
No matter where I go

You will always be there for me
To help me with my last breath
Or pull me from a drowning sea
It is you brother you and me

March 2, 2022

Burning Down Love

I want to be one with time
I want to hide
I want to break down the walls
That holds me inside

I want to touch the flame
That burns the streets today
I want to feel the sunlight on my face
I see the clouds fade

Only to take shelter from the rain
It is building then burning down
Burning down love
And when I go there

I go there with you
It is all I can do
While the city is in chaos
And our love turns

We are blown by the wind
I will show you a place
High above the city of pain
Burning down love

May 14, 2022

By Your Side

It is easy to breathe
When I see the world through your eyes
On my knees
Or by your side

There is no other place to be
It is easy to laugh
When I see you smile
Turning the pages of time

Coming to terms with life
It is by your side that makes this happen
Do what you must
Just do not be gone too long

Because it is easier by your side
It is easy to imagine
When you create a symphony of joy
Like a butterfly dancing in summer air

As long I am by your side
The world is ours to take
Stand before another day
And wish it was another day

March 16, 2022

Calling Your Name

When I fall so too does my heart
Spiraling out of control
On cloud 9
Do not let me go

Or catch me if I fall
These wings are only for show
When I am lost in the storm
I only look like an angel

When I am calling your name
I will wrap you in my wings tonight
Stand you up in the moonlight
There was no turning back

For you are mine in this dark embrace
While we stare at the ground
Nowhere to look around
As gravity pulls us down

Will you catch me when I fall?
I will wrap my wings around you tight
When I am lost in the storm
Still calling your name

March 12, 2022

Cascade Through the Void

I wanted you gone
But I hear you in every sound
Your face in every crowd
Your ghost will not go away

Your presence
Turns my heart to stone
I am left with nothing but fear
I know I am better off alone

My eyes do not need to see
If the sight is to be turned to stone
I will hold my head up high
Cascade through the void

February 19, 2022

Changes In the Mind

Do you think I understand
But I will be fine
Plans we're changed
So, was my mine

Wrong or right
Long nights made bad
How things went sad
Or needing to be strong

It was all in a change of mind
Missed feelings
Behind closed doors
As I gave you more

In place of magic moments
It is best you go
While hating goodbyes
Or knowing why

It is in the coming round
That change minds
And finds us left behind
While the heartache passes

March 2, 2022

Choose A Follower

If my words burst into existence like a sunrise
And my heart touched you
Would you hear my voice come through?
Would you hold it close?

Thoughts are unbroken
All is better spoken
My heart is yours and full
Let there be words to fill the air

Waves in still water
Reaching out my hand
May your cup always be full
For there is a fountain

There is a road paved with light
Between the dawn and the dark of night
If you go no one will follow
That path is for your steps alone

You may choose a follower
And you may fall
If you stand alone who is to guide you?
But If I knew the way I would take you home

May 2, 2022

Cinderella Belly

You carry my child
In your belly so tight
You carry to never get distracted
But I did

As the flames cover the ceiling
So too does my façade
Because I will give you my heart
Despite my soul

This will burn in the ceiling
Till I am done with this
This is the moment I choose
To be honest

I know where this is going
And these fits
I got distracted
But no one knows me as you do

You are one in a million
I will continue to
No faking
I really am going to try this time

March 18, 2022

Clouds Collide

Fetching the moon
Into the night?
Could I have not been good enough
Like season doing their part

It was too much for my mind
So, I walked the line
Or talk about the time
For all this space between us

As the feather out the window, you flew
I slowly sank with the season
Only to get lost in the other
And pretend we do not care

Watching clouds collide
While I sank
And now I find you
In all these big things

No more a shallow man
You gave me a reason
A place to breathe
I know you will not leave me

A way to make it right
Those calls at night
The night can see it
The darkness will be ever good

Never hard to believe
To get lost in each other
And care about it all
Just watch clouds collide

May 2, 2022

Dark Soon

Shadows fall if you wait long enough
Time is running away
I feel like my soul has turned into steel
I still have scars the sun refused to heal

There is not even a place for my soul to be
It will be dark soon and you can find me there
And my sense of humanity too
Behind everything beautiful there is pain

You wrote me a letter so kind
Everything was going fine
I just do not see why I even cared
It will be dark soon and you will find me there

I have lived a hundred lives it seems
I have followed the river and I got to the sea
I have been at the bottom of the world of lies
I stopped looking for the truth in others' eyes

Sometimes my burden is more than I can bear
It will be dark soon and you will find me there
I will live and die here in the dark
It may seem that I am moving but I am standing still

Every nerve in my body is so naked and numb
Sometimes my memory gets clouded
What am I getting away from?
It will be dark soon and you will find me there

May 13, 2022

Day the Earth Stood Still

The youth played possum
The Day the Earth Stood Still
If only they would stand
And the governor was there

In boots and a cowboy hat
The president was an invisible man
So, you know something is wrong
For it is free for all and umbrellas

Everyone is caught up in a tornado
And it is a deadly pace
All this started from outer space
And the youth played possum

May 12, 2022

Dear Me

Dear me
To the man, I used to be
It is in the perception
Where you will find direction

Make decisions wisely
Do not worry about what is behind you
Or in front of you
What's inside the rear-view mirror is closer than it appears

You did your best with what you were given
But you were given time
To make the wrongs right
And be the best you can be

March 3, 2022

Depths of My Soul

You take me to the depths of my soul
The unknown where hands fail
And I find you in the enigma
In so deep

Will my faith stand up?
As I call out your name
To hold my head up high
As tensions rise

I will rest my head in your embrace
For I am Yours and You are mine
Your grace is plentiful in my soul
And your hand will be my guide

Where hands fail and fear surrounds me
You have not failed, and you will not now
Lead me to trust
Let me walk with my soul

Wherever You would call me
Take me deeper than my feet could ever wander
And my faith will be made stronger
I will call upon your name

April 3, 2022

Determined Soul

The wintery chill
Of seasons like never before
Could winter dance any harder?
It seems so out my window

As it beats the window pain
It is so loud I cannot hear
My thoughts touched every second
So, I spend waiting for you

This situation affords me
No second chance to tell you
I wish you were here
Our distance is killing my love

When the warm wind comes again
You will be home at last
No more thousand miles apart
Something deeper brought together

I will remember
Once we were young
No heights could keep us
We had our sanctuary

Always destined for greater things
Never regretting the choices, we made
How many times have I stared at clouds
Thinking that I saw you there

The waiting feelings do not pass so easily
But I always have the love in my heart
Moments lost though time remains
I am so proud of what we have become

No pain remains just love
Eternity awaits
Give me wings so I can fly
My determined soul is longing

May 12, 2022

Different Kind of Pain

Alone in my room
My solitude understands me
It hurt more than it was supposed to
But this emptiness held the key

As I try breathing
A different kind of pain took over me
A deeper loneliness
I act like I know this place

Because I see it on my face
Buried deep inside of me
Shedding a different kind of tears
I bore this skin

Save me from the hell I am in
I will tear out the pages of this story
And not let the heaviness swallow my fight
Because these tears can disappear

March 3, 2022

Drifting Through the Sky

If I wake up without you
Tell me it will be alright
We are going to be
It can only be made in our eyes

Where there is no fight
I am losing my mind
Do not leave me behind
We need a bit more time

Because I don't want the world to turn without you
And I don't want the sun to burn without you
If I lose you my world would stop
And there would be no more sun

Your bravery is not needed all the time
I know you will make it right
You want to do the right thing
It is the truth in your eyes

And I am on your side
I will be here all the time
Loving you to the moon and back
Drifting through the sky

Because I don't want the world to turn without you
And I don't want the sun to burn without you
So, hold me now
Hold me like never before

Do not let go
Give me another minute to lay here in your echo
I don't want to live a life without you
I will watch the world burn without you

May 14, 2022

Dumping This Life

Do not miss your call
For the blood will not wash out
Take sight of your plight
Screaming left in your flight

Retrieval when called
Or leash in agony
No more snow to deal
We parted the sea

To get to the other side
And left you behind
Dumping this life
Because death was looking for me

May 2, 2022

Ego Let Me Go

I will do this for the first time
A moment made no stays in the hand
No limited ways
I am deeper than my labels

No fear left to know
Ego let me go
Get familiar with my ways
I am getting off your merry go round

I am me watch me show you
My new labels now keep up
Truth be told my heart is talking
Fear of the mind is more courageous

Logic and rational creativity
Scratching belief to the surface
As I enjoy my new ride for the first time
Courageously of the heart

January 8, 2022

Ego Trap

Trapping the ego
Egocentric thinking
You with your low frequency
You drain me in your often ways

In my blame, I blame you
So, I know victimization
But I lost my way my source
Closed off energy is my symptom

To be open I would be more than enough
My duty and my recharge
To remain open to the source
Victim mentally is only a development of ego

January 8, 2022

Escape

This is difficult to say
Thought I could keep my PTSD at bay
Behind that diamond ring
You are innocent and all that you bring

Trust me it has been a difficult year
It has been loveless I fear
Deep down I am petrified with fear
If only I could stop screaming and shed a tear

I know you see me in a perfect light
I fake it but deep down I am not right
This perfect façade is falling
And escape is calling

March 28, 2022

Face of Fear

Do you think you are better than the rest of the world?
Think about it why do you fight so hard in your dream world?
You lust for blood like you are in a holy war
While you listen to everyone shout and roar

It is time to make a change
In the end, it is in the range
Time has taken its toll on your face it shows fear
No more fighting on the firing line it is clear

Because change requires a spotter
Did you think you always walked on water?
Did you think you could win this fight?
It is like looking at the sky and a dying star at night

Lies are told and burn up into the dirt
Making moments for the devils hurt
Changing will bring you sooth
Cross into the truth

The wrong way, with the right views
Breaking promises causing blues
Changing is the way to matter
Because you do not walk on water

March 25, 2022

Face the Fiddle

Everyone said I should leave you alone
I cannot move on
This song I sing to the ocean blue
Forever wrong for you

That is how I play it
The remedy for memory
As I face the fiddle
Haunted by the strings

As they play their deadlines
In my dark paradise
And I am too scared to sacrifice
Or wait for the other side

Because I am only comparing it all to you
In closed eyes
So, I will stay here
Even though I should go

February 12, 2022

Fair Dared

It is a story about two men a distance apart
But that shall not take their heart
For love was in their sight
As they walked hand in hand

Only to find they were whole all along
By the streams which carry their fair
To the skies, they wish all they dare
You are my love, and I will love forevermore

February 1, 2022

Faith in me

In blue filled eyes
Mountains can be moved
Sail ocean waves
It is faith in me you see

This love I carry with me
So alive
And carefree
No more lonely night

Or shadows in the dark
Will you walk by my side?
Or carry me if I fall
Even if I must crawl

March 2, 2022

Falling In to Break Out

My desires gave into the flames
The same ones that consumed this town
Could you be the only one to save me?
Or be the one to start the fires

I am falling in just to break out
With you
With me
With a broken heart

February 17, 2022

Figured it Out

It was easy to decide
When you clouded up my mind
It was a fight I would lose
All the time

I could never claim victory
When you always took sides
But I will always have my pride
No, never again

No, not this time
You forced this hand
I thought I know you
But you brought us here

And you know
The truth lies in your eyes
And dripping from your tongue
Boiling in my blood

But I see
What kind of man you are
If you are a man at all
I figured it all out

March 20, 2022

Find Me

Goodbye came so easily
In these words, we made our peace
But this love will not give up
Home is where we will be

Like a river, always running
I keep losing you
Like a fire, always burning
I will be here for you

With an open heart
Just come and find me
Your search for forever is over
Just come and find me

March 5, 2022

Flaws

We may have flaws
Looking at them piece by piece
The perfect mistakes
But still, we are undone

With both of our flaws
As we lie here hand in hand
And inherited the learning curve
That passes from man to man

Only to leave our souls empty
Can you not feel it?
The hole left in your soul
I can feel it

I have always carried this burden
And carried it on my sleeve
So, I bury it in the ground
Only to dig it up again

And see what is left for me to touch
Flaws and all
Yes, I exhumed my flaws
So, I am not doomed

March 5, 2022

Flow Like a River

I am transparent as a river
But now I think I am corrupted
You put bitterness inside me
I have hatred since you stole my identity

No matter how many steps I take
Your mistakes keep coming up
I keep hoping you will come to save me
Your cold heart burns everyone around you

I knew you once and now I cannot speak
I have tried to wash you away
But you just will not leave
So, I do breathing techniques

Dive in deep
To hell with the problem
Focus on the solution
And maybe you will stop haunting me

One day I will be free
To live my life for me
Stop feeling corrupted
And flow like a river

March 29, 2022

Flow Like the River

After a recent grieving
I saw the world in a different way
I had not seen the sun quite the same
It rose above the day to greet the dawn

The earth was covered with life
And storms raged throughout the night
If you listen closely there is a whistle in the wind
My feelings were flowing like the rivers

I think I have this new perception figured out
All this life on land and water
It will find a way to its demise
You have a choice on what you are going to think

And it is there you will learn what I know
All this world will flourish
You must learn to let it go
And flow like the river

March 29, 2022

Forged From Love

It only takes a moment in time
To take a situation
Quickly change it entirely

But promptly acknowledge
Your inner strength
Your bravery to persevere
And demand more of yourself

The burden of growth
Does not come on the backs of luck
It is forged from loving yourself
Commitment and rational thinking

Taking true positive action
Any goal can be met

January 3, 2022

Found Right in Front of Me

You will be the red flag for me
Talking sense to me
My way to focus
So, I do not lose sight

I have moved further
But I have missed you
And you are still my red flag
Talking sense to me

Because I found love
Where it was not supposed to be
Staring right in front of me
Taking my senses from me

Yes, I found you right in front of me
Where you were not supposed to be
I will make it out alive
No matter how hard

I will be bold
Looking to my senses
To get me through
Right in front of me

February 22, 2022

Getting Closer

Sidetracked and run aground
In this spooky place
Bound with spotlights
Phone ringing and text line after line

Walls crack open showing the one in my soul
You take my heart
Yes, your words find my soul
Like the moon, I run

Words cutting at my flesh
Leaving me in the corner as carnage
Driven by your stranglehold
As I open another vein

Only to show no mercy
As it goes again
I close my eyes to not see my torturer
Only to cry acid rain

And bleed dry
Can I blink at the skies above?
When this fire keeps raging inside
He is getting closer

The time is upon me
My bones are feeling his temper
Back to my corner where I left my love
It is still there where I left it

So, I will learn to sleep
In the dream, I will be
Even old I am told I will be bold
All these years of chasing have taken their toll

He is getting closer
It is in his temper
As my flesh leaves my body
He gets closer

January 8, 2022

Ghost Now

The dove flies
So, do you and I
Unbound
Born to run free

Leave this place
To its ghostly shell
And be a ghost no more
A body of aching bones

The chasing of footsteps in the dark
While trumpets play leaving no sound
Who is the ghost now?
Who will walk the streets alone?

When there is something to say
Pat pat as your feet walks away
It is this avoiding me I will not stay
So, be sick of supporting love

It is tainted
It is anchored
Where they shall not look
Like shadows, it was all smoke

My name will not touch your lips
Nor words be spoken
As the moon lights my way
Not to be broken

To do it my way
I do not know why
It is for love
That is what I am doing it for

April 22, 2022

Goodbye Mother

How a moment made it wrong in my brain
Like chemicals rushing through my veins
Feeling flushed and out of control
The pain, the highs, and the lows

Like God needs to take the wheel
And take control
Because I am seeing fire in my soul
Burning up is infuriating me

Just like combustion, I am going to explode
Suddenly, I am confused, and you are all I need
You are my rock
My world my everything

Yes, mother, it is you
I am going to miss you
And I could try to find ways to not hurt
But will miss you

Just one more day with you could I be blessed
Because it is you, mother
My life has been moved and improved by you
I love you

January 13, 2022

Got My Soul

It was in a place I once knew
Only to come back and find my soul
Once lost now found
Hidden the in the ground

Reborn like a rose with no thorn to scorn
My humble in toe like a baby
I love I watch I grow
You are my long-lost soul

Oh, how I have missed you
Even wished and yes kissed you
You brought me more than happiness
You brought me peace

You only need to look into my eyes
To see the tears, I have cried
Or the line on my face
To know the pain I had to take

I was on a journey to come back to you
So, I would know what to do
Only to come back and find my soul
It was in a place I once knew

February 3, 2022

Gravitate

Appreciation comes when we realize
It is in our absence
To explain our worth
Energy should speak for itself

To obsess with proving our worth
Making it hard to truly understand
Gets us caught up in a game
Of validation and depending on others

Become drawn to not loud
Let our presence be powerful
Focus on ourselves
Let good vibes gravitate toward us

January 22, 2022

Happiness

To be happy is a choice
Choose things in life that will make you happy
Decisions that benefit your choices
Enjoy the peace of glee

The art of being happy
Lies deep within us all
In the power of extracting
Happiness from common things

March 25, 2022

Happy And Bright

How the darkness consumed me
Feeling heartless and bitter
But in the light is everything
Brightness and colors all around

The glow back in my eyes
The magic in my soul
I was so lost in the black hole
I am in love with being alive

Dreaming of the light
Seeing in color
Knowing I will be alright
Looking to the skies

I have even found rainbows
On the scariest of days
But it is in the light
I will come out and play

All day I will daydream
Consumed with the right things
In the dark, I realized life is short
So, do not take life for granted

Colorful eyes will play on fields
Not losing hope of what is left of this heart
And I will prevail
We all will see the colors of the rainbow

The scars make us who we are
We will not be lost in the wind
Pick yourself up
Open your eyes and see the light

It will not be scary long
The colors will guide you home
Just come along and play me
Just put the past behind you

The demons will not try to find you
If you put the colors on you
So, let in the light
Be happy and bright

April 3, 2022

Home Again

I am back home
Alone and on my own again
So, I close my eyes and hope again
Going to make it right this time

Be patient and dedicated
More present and giving to life
I am changing it is changing
Time is changing

No standing still
Or giving up
As I search for silence
To write it down

The home creaks to let me know
Close my eyes
Lay my head down
It is time to rest

February 13, 2022

Hopelessness Paralyzed

Hopelessness starts in the heart
To the last beat that lies
In a cold winter chill
Left to walk the earth

In a faded light
Only to give up
Or realize
It has become an uprising

Ripping through the world
Like the great divide
Leaving this soul behind
And I am paralyzed

But the broken come alive
And so too does the light
One breath of life
The sun will shine

Fighting back the flood
We are taking back the earth
Taking back the hopelessness of this heart
For it beats true

March 28, 2022

How Can I

Yes, I am here
so, speak to me
I need to know you feel me
Do you hear me

If you walk away
So does my light
The only place
I found peace

You are my strength
That keeps me walking
I find hope in your eyes
That keeps me trusting

And you shine the light
To my soul
You are my purpose
For everything

It is hard to stand here
And not be moved by you
Nothing could be better
Then this right now

You calm the storms
And you give me rest
You hold me in your hands
You will not let me fall

You be still my heart
And you take my breath away
Would you take my everything in?
Take me deeper now

How can I stand here with you?

March 4, 2022

How Not to Win

Oh, how the argument is won
When you want to be right
The objective is not to win
But to understand

Feel understood
Compromise
On the issue at hand
For it is not a competition

February 14, 2022

Humanity

As the river's stream
And the sun flares
The closer my thoughts
My clouded perception

No longer askew
Invisible Yahweh now visible
Vibrating through and through
Out of the shadows into the spirit

To order the universe
Into the cosmos
Destruction
Genius

Genocide
Humanity
Turned dark
For our rebel soul

A miracle
Forever told
Love forever shown
Bared on the cross

Left an empty hole
Before there was before
He was all
And after his wrath

Still, be his all
Every living being
Will fall and bow before His face when called
It will be the reckoning

April 25, 2022

Hurricane

The morning sun breaks through the night sky
To show the carnage of last night's fall
Shaky and loud recalling the scratches on the wall
So, what is wrong if I died

There will be better days
Give it an inch and feed it well
More days to come, new places to go
I remember asking, when will this ever end?

The hurricane from hell
But I am still here
And the hurricane is gone
No more feeling on fire or ready to shout

March 26, 2022

I Am Good

So, you say
While pain drips from your lips
Can you not let it rest?
The torture you create

It is the depression now
That strangles you
Like hands around your neck
Getting tighter each time you resist

You see your fake as it reflects
Mirror mirror on the wall
To another night you recall
Only to forget it all

Oh, how you wish it would
If only you could be the sane
You work hard
On your hamster wheel

If only you worked that hard on yourself
The tears would not fill up so many jars
But you always say
I am good

March 14, 2022

I Am In

I get confused throughout the day
Because good times come go
Give me some help on what I should say
Because sometimes I just want to walk away

I am looking to understand
Everything has a purpose and a need
So, I am standing here at your door
And I am looking for some answers

I will be honest and true
So, tell me what I am here for
And we can move on
Our future is in front of us

You asked some questions
We need to stay focused
Because I would do this all again
No matter how it goes I am in

May 13, 2022

I Am Not Leaving

Think you can get rid of me
This is my home, and I am not leaving
I will beat back all who try
Think you can steal what little I have

Told to drop my pride
Stop this fight I will never win
But you will not take this from me
I am all alone in this fight

I will take it to the last night
You have no reason why
The winner gets to keep on winning
The words continue to storm

To reach me how it must be
You will not have your way with me
With my finger on the trigger
For all that I have been fighting for

Because it will not matter if I am right
When they come kicking at my door
And the sun meets daylight
Tonight, the rain drowns the worries

While you talk with poison teeth
You will not quit
So, too will I
Just do not touch me

April 1, 2022

I Am Not Sorry

It must have been when the raven landed on my window seal
Because I do not remember the moment I tried to forget
But the tears flowed like a river
I lost myself, is it better not said?

I was so close to the edge of the abyss
In a million emotions tangled in a thousand thoughts
Going down, I was taking everyone with me
The abyss here I come

No apologies and no regrets
Not thinking clearly or sane
Could you save me, if only you could reach me?
One day, maybe we will meet again

Tring to imagine a time of truth, happiness, and peace
Singing a song or dreaming a dream not a nightmare
Could this be my never-ending story?
At the hands of a hate crime

I will pay with my pride
Glory will be mine in the end
If I do not lose faith
Because I will not say I am sorry

March 25, 2022

I Become

I become what I cannot be
When your ways affect me
You lie in the still
While I wait on your will

Could it be in a glace?
Or in a winter romance?
That this is not a chance
To put me in a trance

How this winter kills
As too your eyes chill
To leave in this paralyzed
So, too I will be chastised

Only to be seen without sight
In a lover's eyes delight
Because your ways affect me
I become what I cannot be

March 14, 2022

I Cannot Dream Again

I lie awake in my bed
Thoughts of you running in my head
Alone with these four walls
Imaging the hands of time

To face another day
Distance has a hold on you again
But I will see you soon
And this poem is for you

I cannot dream again
I will have to wake
And miss you all over again
Eyes, I recognize

Familiar to me from some other time
Remembering our times together
Till we can breathe as one
I cannot dream again

March 29, 2022

I Got You

You can rest now
The fight to stay alive is over
My love you
Put up a strong fight

It is all right
Dark days are gone
I am here
I will always be here

I hold you
I will always hold you
Your huge, beautiful heart
It is all right

You will live through me
I will carry on your beauty
We are all right
I have got you in me

You will breathe through me
And calm the storm inside
Just breathe through me
We will keep the candles lite

I will face down the world with you
I am here
I am here always
To hold you always

May 8, 2022

I Had to Leave

I had to leave to find myself
The dripping atmosphere still in my hair
Like summer rain walking under weeping willow trees
Oh, how time never changes

I return so does the moon
Spring, Autumn, winter, and June
But I sailed across the sun you see
Faded into the Milky Way with glee

Showed off to shooting stars
Even showed all my scars
As I looked for myself out there
On a search for a soul

Tracing my way through the constellation
I found more
Reminders of room to grow
And an atmosphere still dripping in my hair

January 19, 2022

I Just Ride

To the open road, I go
Long trucking on wheels of gold
How to hold and sing the blues
Full-time love with a heart of gold

Hot or cold
Nothing will break me down
As I travel
I have been trying too hard

With one pretty poem
Driving too fast
And looking too hard
I am alone in the night

Been looking for trouble
Or maybe trouble will find me
So, I just ride
Dying young and I am playing hard

That is the way I am made
It is the art of life
Drink all day and we talk till dark
Do not leave me now

Do not turn around
Because I am alone in the night
I have trouble with my mind
So, I just ride

March 7, 2022

I Will Be the One

I know that one day
I will be that one
That gets picked
Out of a crowd

Or on a lonely street
I may even meet you through a friend
I will be the one
To make you happy

To keep you laughing
Be your sun on a cloudy day
Life flies by the moon lite
So, too does my love in the midnight sky

Always guiding me by your side
And take picnics
Along with grassy fields
One day I will be the one

March 8, 2022

I Will Come for You

Watch the sands in the hourglass
Will you wait for me?
Because I will come for you
No matter how near or far

This heart is where you are supposed to be
Just thinking of me
When your pride is on the floor
You will be missing me

Then I will turn to you
And fill that space in your heart
So, you can recall that soft touch
That one kiss you cannot forget

And that warm embrace forever stay
If you dream of me
As I dream of you
In a place that is warm and dark

A place where your heartbeats
In my longing for you
And desire
To see your face, your smile

To be with you wherever you are
Just say you will wait for me
To feel my heartbeat more
To be in your arms once more

Where all my journeys end
Just make a promise again
I know it is one you can keep
I promise I will come for you

March 26, 2022

I Will Give

I left it all behind me
No more love for you
This heart is taped out
By the words you said

And the eyes left staring
No more cash
The cards are empty too
What a lesson to learn

When you bring shame to me and you
I got my heart right here
And I have my scars
Bring a cup and bring a drink

I will bring this to fame
I will give it all of me
I will give it all I got
I have confidence in me

April 3, 2022

I will

I will trust you
When you see
The sorrow behind my smile

I will know you are the one
When you can feel
My love behind my anger

I will have faith in you
When you can find
The reason behind my silence

February 18, 2022

If I Am Free

You will not know how I feel
While these four walls close in on me
As blind as I may be
I keep holding on for something more

When all I need to do is walk through the door
I lost my will to fight
There are no answers to find
Maybe I will on the other side

I could fly high above this life
Or far away from this pain
I would face my fears
And just disappear

I would be happy on my own
I could fall in love again
And deal with my broken heart
I can be anything I want to be

And I would never feel my scars
If I am free
I will trust in me
And not lose faith

March 4, 2022

If I Hold My Breath

If I hold my breath
Will it stay this way?
Right here in this moment
In this dream with you

Getting louder now
Can you hear it echoing?
As vibrations in my mind
Will you share this with me?

I want to be here with you
Shining with the sun
All the stars we steal from the night sky
Still, it feels like it will not be enough

No, never enough
As towers fall
We still stand
Just hold my hand

These hands could hold the world
But it still would never be enough
No, never enough
If I hold my breath

March 7, 2022

In Love with the Poem

Sometimes I feel like recognizing my worth
Realizing the man in the man in the mirror
A stranger, caught in memories so long
This place is set in stone

Only to break the chains and go
Leave this state of mind
A demon pulling far from the inside
Life is about to change

Because nothing is going to stop me now
I have been staying here too long
It is time to be where I belong
I am in love with the poem

My heart wants to write
My journey will take me to do what is right
I have done this all my life day and night
Taking the voyage because I am the voyager

I am fortunate to be so content
When you do what makes you happy
The goosebumps and peace you feel
Is better than a sunrise when you are in love

But remember what got me here
Draw upon memories to create
I have got to keep moving for it is too late
I am in love with the poem

Sun shines and so do I
I will shine bright like the brightest star
Magic made in words and roads of thoughts
Flowing softly and silently

Cruel and sad but that is life to grieve
I am with you to listen closely
We might somehow end up together
Dream of the dream little dreamer
I am in love with the poem

March 24, 2022

In My Youth

You look at me and all you see is my youth
Through satellites cruising by
Was it part of the past?
Or are you wishing for a future star?

Signals crossing can get confusing
But just enough to make you feel something
Like a crazy dream
It is enough to make you feel crazy

You will not lose if you play the game
Dress right to play the part
It is work or a coffee shop
Either way, you know where it is at

To be young and get what you want
Love and lust it is never enough
Being young knowing you are the coolest
And the world will refuse you not

Seen it all in a world of blues
Leaving a trail of contributions in your wake
And it is enough to make you go crazy
In my youth

March 23, 2022

In Smoky Shadows

I give permit
You will not find
Your imagination persists
Having no end

I am not the wicked
This end has wicked ways
To its beginning
To its between

Shall your shallowness
Be transparent
For all the world to see
On judgment day

May 4, 2022

In Spite Of

I know how to talk to you
And I know what I want
It is a matter of purpose
Even if I might get distracted

It is only a mirage
One that leaves me embarrassed
But you know me best
You know I exist for you

So, I continually knew
And give it to you
Because I know I excite you
You are pestered by pain

So, let's be honest
And let go of our shame
It is a black cloud
And it is only a facade

It is better to focus on the good
There is nobody quite like you
I hope my words get to you
Now continue to move

Throughout life happily
Do not fake it
I am going to try this time
Going to give you my heart

In spite of my soul
I want your love
It is all floating like a flame
A wonderful scenery

You gave it all hope
And all of this is a circle
There is no one like you
Even the ones before you

This is the moment I choose
Between the hope and the hardest
I am going to try this time
To give you my heart in spite of my soul

May 14, 2022

In Your Arms

In your arms is where I would be
Even if the right is wrong
Let me find death
If life is not in that state

With closed eyes
And a fist held tight
So, my head will fit in your chest
To feel your heartbeat

Feeling all your love
All I ever wanted was you, my love
To see the sun in your eyes
As you smile all the while

March 2, 2022

Incomplete

I cannot think
What you do to me
I am incomplete
Will you ever forgive me?

Look I am on my hands and knees
Begging you, please
My love so can you not see
It is you that all I need

I am here in the incomplete
As I crumble
I may fall
I will risk it all

To feel is to be whole
Will you meet me
Will you see me
I wish to touch you

Yet again in that dark moment
Or on that brightest day
But gone away
Like ocean waves

January 27, 2022

Inner Workings

Welcome to the inner workings of my mind
It has been working overtime
Need to keep the demon off my chest
One touch and I know your kiss

Sweet jasmine when I am on your lips
Fast or slow I will take it all
When you know, you know
I think I dreamed all this before

How you move
The way you talk
It all seems like a distant memory
It feels so real to me

Some other place
Here we are in the back of my mind
Now in the dead of night
I know I have seen your hazel eyes

Woke up dizzy
Close my eyes
It feels so real
I think I dreamed all this before

May 7, 2022

Into the Light

Love into the light
Yet the wrong is what comes out right
Leaving me weak
But my muscles burn from the workout

Because I have been working through the lies
Avoiding my soul through the devil's eyes
Trying to gain control of my life again
Would I live that life in sin?

So, I go into the light
As a sinner I am
Holding my prayer up to the sun
Heaven knows what I have done

February 14, 2022

Jealous Sea

You always find a way to keep me in a jealous sea
Everything is right, everything is wrong
Feeling like I am drowning in this jealousy
I will conjure thoughts of you

As I wear this heavy ring
Only to get drunk
Being in love to fight
So, nothing makes sense

Now there is no way to stop the jealous sea
When it comes and I cannot breathe
Rushing over me
Leaving me confused

What do you need?
When you look at me like you do
Do not leave
I just cannot get enough

When everything is right, it feels wrong
So, call my name
As time ticks on
While we are standing here

With the mess we created
But nothing makes sense anymore
But started this jealous sea
When it comes, I cannot breathe

April 1, 2022

Just Like We Do

The nothingness
It is easy to feel it
When we just stand here
Saying nothing

I do not want to go there
I just do not want too anymore
Because loneliness is here with us
We just need to leave

Let it be in our minds if anything
Everyone feels lonely sometimes
I do know-how
Let us go back to good

You do not owe me
And I do not owe you
But things will work out like we want them to
If we see it through

Give us some room to grow
Figure out what to do
There is only love left here for us
Just like we do

February 27, 2022

Keep Doing This

Why do I keep doing this?
You gave me love to bliss
I tossed it away
Should I be left insane?

Only converse with me
What to say I leave on the shelf
Why did I let you go?
Only to holding and not know

It is on left
You realize what a theft
But you have to lose
To know what Is close to you

January 28, 2022

Keep Me in Your Memory

I had a feeling I was missing
Scared and afraid
No one would listen
Or even cared

Feeling a fear
That woke up all my senses
I hope I will be
Remembered for the good

The right
The positive contributions
Try to forget the wrong
Help me to be missed

So, I can be
Remembered for the good
Keep me in your memory
And not be afraid

February 22, 2022

Keep My

To a weakened heart
You took piece by piece
As you ponder on your thoughts
Only to keep me from sleep

If I could only breathe
And see what you see
You push my demons to the surface
And my secrets too

Why did you take their side?
Leave me to the underworld
May I find peace here
Caught in my memories

You have taken my breath from me
You can keep my secrets
All the pieces of my heart
And my demons too

March 31, 2022

Kiss Me

You guys look so cute together
As we sleep eyes peek to gather
Sucking the oxygen from the room
We will not hide we plan to groom

My flesh desires your touch
To have your presence means so much
You want to touch my face
To take me straight to outer space

Nights with a bed of roses
Days showered in proposes
You cracked my code and left nothing to chance
No more strangers or awkward glance

The mode is shifted we broke the mold
No more rainy days to unfold
So, kiss me at the alter
When I am melting and need you my Rock of Gibraltar

Yes, kiss me with your eyes open
They dilate when you see my soul scope in
So, kiss me when I am close
You do not know when you will get another dose

Making memories until days past
As we follow this path at last
We keep each other on track
A little crazy I am always a wisecrack

You are my life I live for you
Now in paradise, you live for me too
Staying together forevermore
How could anything be better?

So, kiss me I just love you
As I melt when you pass through
I will always be at your side
I can count on you with pride

September 9, 2021

Leave Me to Waste

A vail to cover the night
The cold chill in the air
It is you that fades away
My bedroom to the stairwell

Your steps keep me awake
Do not leave me to waste
I am a man of dignity and grace
Slipping through your cold embrace

You could have dropped the bombs gently
Or sympathy in compassion
Because my loneliness builds in your steps goodbye
So, leave just let me down gently

I am left in cold drags of feet
As I'm walking down the corridor
Do not leave me to waste
I am a man of dignity and grace

May 3, 2022

Leaving This Love

I see you calling
When I tell you to leave me alone
It is three in the morning
And you still have not paid my bill

Because you are broke
Looking for money
So, get your foot off my gas
I saw this as to finish line

Stared deep into your eyes
You went too far
Messing with my head
So, I messed with your heart

I have to leave before you love me
Because I know this all too well
I have to leave the party behind
And catch my ride

January 29, 2022

Left Behind

As the violence hits the atmosphere
I tell myself I will be alright
You will be
Maybe this one will not last long

It is an eye for an eye
And I do not know if I
I want you to fight
I am losing my strength to be strong

I am losing my mind
Will I be left behind?
I just need more time
I do not want the world to turn without me

Locked away to never see the sun
My bravery is not calculated
No one is measured on who wins or loses
It is a lie for a lie

And I am getting tired
On this side
I am losing my mind
I do not want to be left behind

March 8, 2022

Left Worsen

Even though the rain was taking my night
Leave me no road to flight
As I walked you pulled up to take me in
Could I have known it was a smile that did me in?

So, you asked my name
Fate should have stopped us with shame
Because it was love at first sight
We will stay with this all night

Making love to you
Saying no only feels the blue
All I want to do is make love to you
Put my arm around you and hold on to you

Your place will do well that night
We did everything right
I could not have been more of a person
But in the mid hours of the night, I felt worsen

So, walked back out slowly
Amongst the gardens and the tree lowly
Hopping not to be found again
Just a memory in your brain

January 18, 2022

Lessons To Be Learned

Lessons to be learned
Bitter love gone
Forgotten light
It is dishonest by itself

Laughter as it passes
Slipping through the fingers
Forgetting all the kindness
As embarrassment covers

To show the pity
Or the shame
What is lost is left alone
Every step forgotten

But try and try again
In time goodwill cut
Trouble never thought
Could never think

How it should not get this bad
As problems hit the floor
Or why they look the same
There are lessons to be learned

March 31, 2022

Letting Go is Easier

Easy to lose your way
Easier to just let go
Cannot tell somebody
Harder to just let them know

You could call
But you do not
Never played this game
Played with my heart so hard

I am not torn about it
Because it was real to me
Wonder do you know how it made you feel
Do you remember how you let yourself feel?

Could there be a stay in your heart?
When letting go is easier
I will keep the secret though
No one needs to know

February 21, 2022

Life's Big Meaning

Life has a big meaning
It is bigger than you
Even though you are not me
There are lengths you will go to

To see the distance in their eyes
It is a warning
I am pale in my virtue
But I am in the spotlight

Losing thoughts
Trying to keep up with you
But I do not know if I can do it
Listen to my words

Till the last one is spoken
As you hear them
Refrain from laughing
Just try

You will hear whispers
Every waking hour
So, choose them wisely
I will keep an eye on you

Like a blinded fool
That brought you to your knees
And all this was a fantasy
And just a dream

May 14, 2022

Light I Fight to Be

In the dark I long
And in the light, I fight to be
As I wear my mask so shadows cannot see
Darkness covers me

Putting pieces of the puzzle together
Missing piece I yearn to find
As the torture covers my mind
The truth will mock me still

Because life is near
The darkness will come
The light I will fight to be
For I am seeing hope

To not stand alone
Take my hand
And pull me from the dark
No more secrets left to hide

February 13, 2022

Listen Closely

In my days of youth
I found days that looked better
Told troubles will pass
And find someone to fall in love

Take your time do not live too fast
Listen closely to these words
They will help in the end
The universe is working for you

Be a simple man living a simple life
Do what you love and believe in
It is a simple life where happiness is
Everything you need you possess

February 27, 2022

Live My Life

I am too busy moving
Moving as fast as water flows
Tears that make no sense at all
Life is happening

Where plans are made
And you cannot stand at all
I choose to live life every day
Say what people never say

I will take all the love and all the pain
Because I will live this life today
Strong and confident I can take the pain
Even these turns in my way

They are faded signs ahead
But life happens I have plans
Step to the right just do not stand
I will live my life today

March 30, 2022

Locked Away

The passes in a daydream
Locked away never finding a thing
As I search
Not learning a thing

Words meaning nothing
While I keep my dreams tightly
Telling no one
Because you never say I love you

Will I ever know what it is like to hold you?
If only I could look into your mind
What would I find?
the uncertainty

to drop your guard
or show your heart
life can be so unkind
to a broken heart

February 12, 2022

Look and a Kiss

You took me down to the count
With a look and a kiss
As sweet as watermelon bliss
Yes, I want to touch you again

With soft caresses
And a genuine drive
Underneath the stars
Yes, I want to touch you again

It was a feeling like that
That makes a kiss like that
Have me come to life like that
The fire all day and all night

Wishing it would never end
Yes, I want to touch you again
Up close and all right
Till the sun goes down

And the moon lights up
It is you I want all day and all night
Because you took me down to the count
With a look and a kiss

January 26, 2022

Looking For a Reason to Live

I fight the fight
And I look to your reason
You have a way of making me see
Your side all the time

I try to tell you mine
It is not worth the fight
I am winning a losing war
The one you put on me

I start nothing
All I do is love and live
To be free in my world
Did I hurt you along the way?

No did I not so why all this war
You bring on me
I react to your hate
Then I am the bad guy

Why so unfair the hate
So, I look for a reason to live
In all this hate
No one to hold me when I am

In this hard case
Too much time to find me
Yet never do in all this hate
I look to find a reason to live

So, I stay here
I am to belong
It is me, lord
Why not see that I am here?

April 1, 2022

Lose To Learn

It is time ticking away
Like summer rain tonight
But it is a landslide of emotions
Everyday

One more minute I will feel better
I will think of you no more
And no more remembering
No more feeling numb

I am feeling everything
I had to lose to learn
Words escape me
It is a flame till it burns

Then it hurts till it eats you alive
Changes you forever in the blink of an eye
It does not fade overnight
It stays with you for your life

May 12, 2022

Lost And Found

Sometimes you must get lost
If you want to be found
Look at yourself in the mirror
It is an illusion of time

The distance between the past and the future
And you can count it by the faded scars
Your abandoned hope
And is not good enough

Has less to do with who you are
And more to do with who you can be
As the voices persist
Your imagination will exist

So, try to reshape them
Let them radiate through you
Do not let the world bitter you
Share your happiness be true

March 30, 2022

Lost And Ripped Open

To be ripped open
Parts missing
Feeling numb
Tired of trying

Moving in one place
Tears fall like rain
Lonely is my days
In the corner, I cry

So, no one hears
You cannot touch me
Or hold me
I want anyone at arm's length

The night is my only comfort
I shall be nowhere else
I will stay in the dark
I will make it on my own

No one needs me
And I need no one
I am lost
And ripped open

May 13, 2022

Lost In Memories

I just stay lost in memories
I cannot recognize the real me
A stranger caught in the past
As if my place is set in stone

Chained to this commemoration
Demons pulling far from the inside
A change must change
Before it changes me

I must break the shackles at daybreak
For I have been here too long
This is not where I belong
It is alright to walk alone

I must take a risk
As the sun rises so do I
I will go where I belong
I will end up at home

April 3, 2022

Lost Your Body

Breathless
Sleepless
My mind is on your spine
Thinking and thinking

In all mine
Is it over?
To let me love thee
To hold thee

It will murder me
If I lost your body
Breathless
Sleepless

February 13, 2022

Love Enough to Fight

I come for you
All these miles
To find you
Will you find me

In this fight, we find each other
The struggle we work through
You make me
And break me

Still, I long for your existence
And you have mine in yours too
Love enough to fight
So, you lose nothing you gained

No broken hearts
The best of hearts
We will love for life
Use us up for life

March 12, 2022

Love Has Died

My eyes have seen love
My heart has felt the beauty of it too
So, I enjoyed the luxury of it all
It told a story for one and all

I was not spared witnessing love's death
In the tragedy, there is nothing left
But in this thought do not forget
I was not prepared for the end

The mirror reflects the truth
When you made up your mind
That love has died
If only you could get out alive

Victimized by the hurt that is gone
Because forever is not for everyone
What has been done is written in stone
For my eyes have seen love's death

There is nobody and there is nothing left
So, do not forget
The end was my time to see
But this is what it looks like to me

March 22, 2022

Madness

I am not a victim
So, I shall not complain
I will accept my faith
Accept my situation

I shall change my circumstances
Remove me from the situation
Staying in the environment
Is pure madness

February 14, 2022

Magnified In the Silence

Justified in what you put me through
It is only a reflection now
Just to fall away
Or close my eyes

Was I liberated?
It is my reflection looking back at me
Why do I deserve this silence?
I did not see this pride in this place

I do not need this space
It is only a reflection
Looking back at me
Take me back

Or take my place
But it is an amplified silence
In a magnified silence
Because it is only a reflection now

March 17, 2022

Main Man

I am the one you call for a good time
I never ask but your husband must not be giving it
It worked for a time
I even got paid, not like a prostitute

You wanted me to last past your main man
You said just hold out just a little longer
Little longer turned into years
I was just a pretty face, who could help you

Get yourself together at your own pace
You were stringing me along
And you misunderstood me all along
High risk and no gain

I am a fool to love the pain
A fool to fall in love
And believe you would ever leave
Still, you call, and I say come over

I am a fool to love the pain
Now, who is your main man?
I get no answer...
So, on the next call, I am not there anymore

Now you are blowing my phone up
Because you realize what you lost
Your main man, in this insane world
I am the one you will not call for a good time

May 13, 2022

Make Love to the Night

Looking up from underneath
Fractured moonlight on the sea
Reflecting on my mode
As I go under a peaceful spell

Breathing in deep the night air
No need to pray, no need to speak
A thousand miles under you
I found a place to rest my head

And all this devotion was rushing over me
The arms of the night are carrying me
So, I rest my head on my thoughts
Make love to the night

March 28, 2022

Memory and Soul

Memories with mass
With electronic charge
Electricity with electrons
Electrons with mass

We are more than our memories
Born with none
Die with more
Then a lifetimes worth

The soul
When we talk about the soul
Memories are the soul
Electrically charged mass

Life is a perception
Many memories change
Defy rules of explanation
We redefine remind

But only when we engage
In the act can we participate
To build and benefit from
That perception

January 17, 2022

Mine To Take Back

In a heart filled with love
I gave to you willingly
I only gave more than I could
Yes, I left nothing for myself

I gave you all that I have inside
And you took my love
As the mirror looks at you
You should have listened to me

And what I believed
It is the words of wisdom
That love will not last
Even though I gave it to you

It will be mine to take back
I only gave more than I could
I gave to you willingly
In a heart filled with love

March 12, 2022

Mirror of Truth

Your insults do not offend me
Personally, I will not take them
For it shows your view
Negative and true to you
How rotten the qualities you possess

The mirror will state your business
Regardless your reality

But I will hear your words
And release my defenses
For I owe no explanation
Nor a nasty reply

Instead, I assess
I realize who I am
And who brought the words
Could qualities like that be in my life

January 8, 2022

Mistakes And All

Waters as clear as the glass you can see the bottom
Seeing the sunrise above the horizon
Aurora shifting at the speed of light
I can see you through it all

There is more to life I know
I have all I need and my blessings
At that moment fear is gone
To say forever

And mean it
For there is nowhere I would rather be
To make mistakes
Waste time

Because you are my future
When you are around, I see it all
Looking in the mirror I see you
Seasons may change

You know where I will be
My heart is right here
To keep making mistakes
Wasting time

Making better days
Learning, living, and loving
We will go as the wind blows
Forever is forever

And forever is what I mean
Because there is nowhere, I would rather be
Mistakes and all
Making memories with you

April 24, 2022

Monstrosity

With your bloodshot eyes
And beer breath
It is the balcony you plan
To put your hands all over me

Violate and control me
I love you comes from your lips
But it is empty
Like your soul

As my pull is tugged to and fro
I cannot getaway
There is not a single reason
For me to stay

Only to wish I could fly
Yes, I will get high on hope
Or mess me up until the morning
All I feel is the numb

Reflecting at me
There has got to be somewhere
Somewhere I can run
To get away from this monstrosity

Stop living this life in purgatory
Fly away and leave this balcony
Bury these memories
That has been holding me down

March 11, 2022

Mother

Now the world can be themselves
You taught no one is better than anyone else
Who needs to think that over?
She did it to me

She did it to you
Make a joke and you will be free
Or get on your knees
To face your God

You will find the love of a mother
The mother's love
It is there in her arms
Coming from her heart

Ready for love, not war
But always ready for more
Never knew anyone more ready before
Who needs to think that over?

Or figure it out
Mother is there to untangle it out
The bigger problem
The better the solution

So, get off your knees
Stand face to face with mother
You will find out who you are
Love and loved by mother

That came from the heavens above
To name you who you are
Love you with open arms
A loving heart and soul

Now you know who you are
Given the love and power of mother
You are more than just a person
No longer disillusioned

January 13, 2022

Must Be Your Way

I caught a shooting star
I made a wish by far
It is in the words it shall come true
Moving fast or slow I will be with you

Dance the dance
To perceive the perception
Now the rain is falling
The truth is bittersweet

As my voice calls out to you
And introduces sweet innocence
Now I ask you to stay
It must be your way

February 14, 2022

My Best Memory

You were my best memory
My love when the world is so cruel
But I spent my time and shallow sheets
I should have seen your intentions

I did not see the signs
I was too busy listening to the words
And lost where I belong
In the love and growing old

Now I am alone
Knowing that all along
You took my warmth and soul
Now I am left here in doubt

And walking in the cold
Is this where I belong?
Gone are days of innocence
Nowhere to hide from me

No one told me how hard it would be
To carry on
When everything is gone
You do not know-how

These days are longer now
My nights spent wondering why
You were my best memory
My love when the world is so cruel

March 7, 2022

My Dreams

Like the sweetest of dreams
You crept into me
To be intertwined
But demons hold you

Crazy when they are not on you
Love on your mind when you call my name when it is in your veins
But I will only turn away
Because when you are down

I will be nowhere around
My whole world is upside down
And you can stay down
The hold has you

Stronger than the grip of my mind
Savior, I am not
Leaving me in doubt
This is not where I belong

I do not recognize you
We are no longer intertwined
You have crept out
Not even in my dreams

April 23, 2022

My Love

Your calls will go unanswered
My heart clicks the clock away
Because you would not see it my way
Or fall to the prayer

Sparks die when you wait in the late
Or hang on to the shame
It is done in this way
I will not give it away

My love no way
No way you will see me crawl
My love this is in ashes
So, dust to dust

February 14, 2022

My savior

I do not need a savior
I saved myself decades ago
My completion is done
I am whole right here alone
I want someone adventurous
Interesting and funny
Kiss me when I least expect it

February 18, 2022

My Strength Will Rise

Countless times the words have been spoken
Many tears have been cried left broken
In moments cutting my feelings to the bone
I stay just like a drone

My time invested makes it easy
Complicating my mind causing doubt and queasy
We have better places to belong other than the thunder
Just listen to the words we both have fallen under

For worse or better we cannot deny our embrace
We belong here in this space
Words escape me when I look into your eyes
But if my strength would only rise

To break the habit
Or distort the facts like a rabbit
Now there is no turning back
And forward is on track

Close your eyes try to sleep
Close your eyes count sheep
Clear your mind and lay
Wash the pain away

March 24, 2022

My Thoughts

Left with my thoughts
As the walls close in
Words you cannot take back
But you say them anyway

You had your demons
And I made them mine
It was a kindred spirit
Intertwined trying to break free

If only the ties that bind would break
In these thoughts we make
You were my nemesis
But I worked on you anyway

Why did you fight me so hard?
And leave me with my thoughts
Could you not see my heart?
Or were you too busy looking at my soul?

March 18, 2022

Naming Stars

We had days of love and hate
Where our minds gave into fate
It was all perfect mistakes
Walking the tunnels and cracks

Under the streets
Excited and got our treats
The search persisted
Sun would rise we were twisted

Looking for ways to get out of this town
Because we were tired of being around
Or was it done with us
Remembering back why make a fuss

Sleeping in other friends' homes
Searching for our personal Sherlock Holmes
Smoking cigarettes
Talking California wildly and jets

Never looking back
The future was our goal no slack
Growing up was our mission
If only we could be older than a magician

Swore we would never die
We would grow old eye to eye
Yeah, swore we would never die
Night falls on the beautiful sky

But we walk the streets
Curfew is short on our receipts
But we talk till the moon tells us it is time to retreat
Dancing in the street

To the music in our heads like superstars
Naming stars
We had days of love and hate
Where our minds gave into the fate

March 15, 2022

Need To Get Away

I will say it to you a thousand times
No matter how many times we go
You are the only thing that is right
So, I push on with what I have done

You are my vision, my light
And every time I look at you
I know we will make it anywhere
But we need to get away from here

Light up the road and never look back
As if we have a choice
Even if you cannot hear my voice
I will be right by your side you

Louder
We will run for our lives
I will speak clearly
Understand

There is no need to raise your voice
I will still see those eyes
And you will not cry
So, we can say our goodbyes

May 14, 2022

Need You

Waited for the right time
The right time never came
To tell you how I feel
I tried countless times

To tell you how I needed you
Here I am without you
Lost and all alone
Bottled up with a heart full of love

Confusion settled over me like a dark cloud
You said goodbye to me in the rain
And I crumbled when the thunder crashed
Because all my life I felt this way

I just did not know how to say
If only you would stay
I would have you to hold
And I would not want to give up

March 29, 2022

Never Let You Go

Emotions in a sunrise
Through a blue sky
I turn to you
As we play in the summer air

Running wild with you
As thoughts go through my mind
But I will never let you go
I am lost in these summer nights

Lost in your warm light
And even when this night is day
I will hold the words I say
I will never let you go

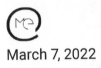

March 7, 2022

New World

I am waking up my mind
Improving cognitive thinking
Breathing in knowledge
Breaking in thought processes

Defining my perception
Because there is no end
The one thing about learning
There is always more to learn

I am waking up; I feel it in my soul
The enlightenment has brought me a goal
This is my new world
Bring on this dreamworld

I have achieved a level of happiness
Completing a revolution
I will wear a hat and fit right in
The goal is set, and the universe will hold me tight

Deep in my soul, straight from inside
I am waking up my soul
It is enough to set a goal
To a new world

March 27, 2022

No More Pretend

Leaving it is what you do best
But you should have stayed gone
I can forgive but forget
Coming back is not in the cards

Because since you have been gone
I dedicated my time
To moving on
It is more about me

No more phone calls
Or hear you say
Keep your promises
I know what you are going to say

Because that is all you will hear me say
I had heard it all before
For the first time, I can breathe again
And I get what I want

No more fighting
You could have tried
But you just wasted time
Thanks to you I am moving on

April 1, 2022

Not Alone

As I fade into the abyss
Lost and afraid
An empty hand in a cold world
With distant light

Could someone save my life?
Or hear my cry
Will you save me now?
You call out to me

In a carry me through it all
Leave no stone unturned
Even catch me when I fall
I have wanted to let go

But you tell me no
Because I am not alone
Mending my broken dreams
And restoring faded memories

Balancing out pain with happiness
Bringing me from the abyss again
Ending the pain
The comfort you bring so close in reach

As you say you are here
With me always
To carry me through it all
And catch me when I fall

For I will not let go
Because I am never alone
You are my hope when it feels all over
And when the world feels shattered

I know your arms will hold me
Love and embrace me
You are with me always and forevermore
To carry me through lives door

January 13, 2022

On and On

So, you started with a goosebump
Then make my head jump
At home between these satin sheets
Locked skin and head feeling repeats

Room service or we will not eat
I am down for all your heat
Day and night drunk on you
Keeping you here cuckoo cuckoo

Even when I am good, I am bad
So, this summer loving looks mad
Touch my body
Because you have the perfect body

So, if you put it on me
We will be together to agree
Swear a long life
Making love not strife

So, if you love me right
It will go all night
On and on
You are the perfect turn on

April 1, 2022

One Minute to Hold

I love more today
Then I loved you yesterday
I will love you more in one minute more
From minute that just past

But in the end
I will find you in my soul as one to know
My one true love I will hold
Because you are mine

February 1, 2022

One More Time

I aligned my courage with the stars
But you still left
How light carries on endlessly
Even after death

Did you not teach me anything?
As my breath grows shorter
You teach me the ways of infinity
And how precious life is

But it bears repeating
Just one more time
How the words come from your lips to my ears
That the universe was made just to be seen by my eyes

Could you say it just one more time?
I would write it down, but I forgot a pen
So, say it just one more time
How the universe was made just to be seen by my eyes

I still have a shortness of breath
While you try to explain the infinite ways
And how rare life is
Could you say it one more time?

March 23, 2022

Only God Knows

Sees you when you are down
Depressed and all around
Crying and upside down
Shy and afraid

When you want to die
Sees you when you smile
It takes a while
At least you are here

He sees you
You are never alone
Sees you when you hide
He sees you in the light

Even in the dark
Within a blink of an eye
He sees you when you think
He even knows all your scars

Yes, he sees you
You are not alone
He sees you when you chase
Even when you run

When laughter comes from fun
Even bitterness comes off your tongue
He sees you
Hoping you will see yourself

January 19, 2022

Peace In a Kiss

I am so happy that you are in my life
I went to bed with the love you share with me
It gives me peace
Comfort to sleep so soundly

And when I wake
I found a kiss so softly touch my cheek
I know it had to be you
I love you

February 1, 2022

Peace in This Place

I will keep you safe
Take shelter in the light
There is peace in this place
Even where monsters hide

There is no such thing as an easy target
He knows everyone here
Even when you do not know yourself
Just let go of the past

Every minute will last
You cannot escape who you are
Or outrun who you are
It is in your DNA

March 23, 2022

Phoenix from the Ashes

I could say more
But why when you are not listening
Every word ignored
As I pick the broken pieces off the floor

Losing my voice as I call on you
There is a shakiness in it

I have been bending till I brake
Watching all these dreams go up in smoke

I will be a phoenix
And come out of these ashes

February 27, 2022

Pick Up the Pieces

As I breathe in
I cannot find words
But you use one
To blow my mind

Making my heartbeat
Faster and louder
For it is a bitter pill
With no one to love

Inside this union
Your corroded heart
Like a world ending
Echoing news louder

As if to drown you out
But it breaks my heart
To see you in pieces
As if no morning will come

Or no daybreak in sight
Just remember you are loved
And pick up the pieces
Mend your broken heart

March 2, 2022

Power of the Mind

If we go
We cannot turn back now
For something
Or something now

You just trip if I push too hard
Anticipation
Let us waste no time
In these useless discussions

Focus on the now
On whatever is trying to take
Cancer in its dying ways
Lost too many to count the ways

Instead, explore the fallen ones
To my special group of friends
For getting me through crazy times
And late nights

The devil testing me
I got my space right
Left in doubt
But power is great

April 25, 2022

Pride

Giving me up
It will not be easy
Realizing you need me
You hold me

I know the lies you keep
I will be by your side
Always
And you do not even know

Till you catch an eye
Passes by sideways
So, I am waiting
In the dark

When the lights are off
In the shadows
Let the fears turn over
Then I will rise

I will be older
Wiser and enough
Choose me
I am left on your shoulder

In your eyes
Getting colder
You will know
To walk away

From those sideways eyes
For I wait no more
I am coming out of the dark
No more waiting

I have been here all along
To be with you
You hold me
Realizing you need me

April 24, 2022

Rainfall

A lot of sensation in it
To feel your skin being rinsed
How blood and sweat go away

Ease the pain of a muscle ache
No more tension or bellyache

Relaxing down to your bones
As impurities wash away

Filling your lungs freshly
You're first breath of the day
As it eases your heart away
To fill your veins

The sound calming your memories
Each drop takes away the wrongs
To replace it with hope
And new beginnings

January 4, 2022

Ricochet

Say all you want
I cannot hear you say those words
Talking so loud saying so much
How you shout it all out

The words will not go to my ears
If you talk so loudly
I know you criticize me
But you did know how it ricocheted

Thought you shut me down
But I got up in your last scream
It was bulletproof I had to lose you
So, try to tear me down

I am more than you know
Try and shoot me down
I am stronger than you think
Do not worry I will not fall

I am stronger than you think
Cut me down
Who is it that you think I am?
This is my world I will show you

Rise to call and the voice
Stones will be my love as bones
As I talk loud saying too much
I am bulletproof with nothing to loss

So, fire away
I will ricochet your hate
Try and shoot me down
I will rise with my strength

April 1, 2022

Rise Again

Together forever
On the day we met
As you slipped through fingers
On the day truth came out

You found false judgment
I want you to stay away
As I rise to take my place
I still see your face

And I am a slave to the shadows
In the forever
You slipped through my fingers
But look what we have become

Now there is empty space
Nothing for me here
I will rise again
I get a dose of my own sins

Our fates collided
But you are someone else
There is just empty space
I will rise and love again

May 6, 2022

Rise to Speak

Will you hear me speak?
Or welcome my words
I should not be afraid
But I am when I am silent

So, I will rise to speak
Even higher
Remembering
I was not meant to survive

February 13, 2022

Rise Up Tall

Dreams insight
Can be achieved day and night
Unleash the beast within
It is time to make believers out of them

Crush the demon team
While you grab it all
Rise up tall
It is a challenge

And you will not fall
Whispers of fear
But listen to the desires
Doubt will stop your progress

This is not where you need to be
Defeat the fallen ones
Live like everything matters
Straight to the top

May 1, 2022

Rock Bottom

Just when I think I hit rock bottom
I wake up with dirt in my mouth
Years lost
Mortgage gone

Worlds gone to hell
Could I choose a worst day to wake up?
So what I got knocked down
Dragged out and bet around

But with every door that closes
Another one opens
Hope to clear my head
And clear my heart

Get rid of these bad days
Because I can move
Stretch out my arms to the sky
I will always be able to reach you

Sweet and pure
As beautiful soaring through the light
In everything I do
Not giving up

As you lift me up
And carry me through
These rock-bottom days
Into what is right

January 25, 2022

Run

To a place other than here
Fresh air flows in natural ways
Could the feeling be more in this moment?
As the sun's rays burn against my skin

To bring newfound fragility to my wounds
Strength turning to vulnerability
Paralyzing so I can realize my loss
I cannot do this anymore

As I shake for no food is left in me
Looking to the mountains to climb
Only to feel the fatigue left in my departure
Get me out of here

Where to look
I do not know
How do I get there?
Appreciating what is gone

With loss comes rebirth
But with nothing bright headed my way I am stuck
Never guaranteed happiness
We create our happiness

But what if I have lost too much
A dream comes true but disappears
So, I stir
And I bookmark my page and look to tomorrow

Asking for a minute more
The heart is suffocating
I ran
Will this new destination be better?

January 6, 2022

Rushes Out My Mouth

Open eyes to the sky
Clouds only embrace
Beating sun rays
Dark in the night

To give grace
Could I be on the right track
Because I cannot see straight
Lost on pavements

Moving past you like a snake
The dark reaches out to comfort me
Reckless in its anger
As it rushes out my mouth

Will I feel your gratitude?
Or will I forget you like I always do
Bury my head in the sand
Words that resonate

Making love all day long
Wisdom hanging over my head
I now know where I am going
My vision is clear

I walk the pavement
And move like a human
I see the light
I reach as it touches my soul

Hope and happiness
As it rushes out my mouth
Grateful
I will not forget you

For the bluest of sky
And clouds to embrace
The sun's rays will shine
To bring on all its grace

May 5, 2022

Sanctuary In My Room

I have a sanctuary
In my room
Away from the sounds
And where time stands still

In a world of imagination
Without intimidation
As the morning comes soon
So, too does the thoughts bloom

So, I stay laying there
In my in between light
Waiting for darkness
Or a better conscience night

How I have become a slave to these events
But it is in my room I disappear
Only you exist here
Sanctuary in my room

January 23, 2022

Say Goodbye to the Old Me

My tongue forms the words
As my lips let it slip
Only to lose my grip
On what I thought I hold

Leaving me wanting more
It is just an ache inside
That I just cannot hide
I cannot hold back

For a life, I know I deserve
In a world of sometimes
Or asking why
Because I cannot just get by

I am on my knees begging
As I hear that voice inside
Could it be telling me lies?
Will my dreams come crashing down?

Or burn up in flames
No more childish ways
I will be the one
I will not be denied

For I will overcome
And stop this hurt inside
But it will take time
So, I am not begging

I am standing up and free
I will stare you in the eyes and be
Believing there are no more lies
And taking it straight from the heart

It is time for a new start
Because if it is not love
It is not enough
I deserve more

And the inside voice is screaming
Get off your knees your dreaming
So, I reach inside
And say goodbye to the old me

March 25, 2022

Seeing Freedom

It is in the things I can accept
I will not worry about the things I cannot change
But take valor in the things I can change
And wisdom is the difference

Years bring in a new age
Even though I thought nothing could change me
I was not listening to anyone
And no one was hearing me

But you continued to affect me
Confusion taking over
I was not thinking anymore
Even though I said I was

All I could think I did not want anyone
Or anymore
Because of bad experiences
But now I feel so different

I have not seen freedom before
I never thought I would make it to be here
Do not let me forget
I want to hold on

March 5, 2022

Show Up

We are more
Then our thoughts
Then our emotions
It is in the realization

Where we come to know
Our center of pure essence
Existing beyond the moment
Beyond the confusion

Past the stress
Time has come to refocus
Lean deep into yourself
Surrender to compassion

Trust the universe
To complete the cycle
Into the new you
As you show up

The role will be played
For the true heart
The authentic heart
Will guide you to reality

January 9, 2022

Side By Side

Your eyes look empty at times
If only I could look through them sometimes
Your plans undone
But has only begun

Take time for a while
Put on a smile
Pass through the silence vail
Without fail

You are not alone
Because promises are known
Coming through the darkness true
Secrets kept too

Even though you were a loner
You were loved more than any owner
Always dreamed of something better
Walking side by side was all that matter

April 2, 2022

Sinner's World

Traveling to my low
Dragging out this love affair
No one is counting
It is always the same number on the door

This tryst causes a scene
Nobody saw it coming
But the little devil in me
Forever drops from your lips too fast

Play the game you get played
Do not blame the player
It is a sinner's rules in a sinner's world
I am what I am

I do not break another heart
It is not worth getting into deep
Or feeling cheap
It is a sinner's world

March 26, 2022

Sleepless With the Shadows

Sleepless
In a world that sleeps
Watching shadows dance
And call me

Beckoning
Who knows what's right?
As the lie gets thicker
My age should make me wise

But I stay awake
Could I say more?
Would it change your mind?
I should give up

But something in me resists
Just give up
This condition is not that simple
There is nothing left for me to say

In a world that knows sleep
Until you can empathize
Giving up now
If only it were that easy

Giving up now
Below, my soul
I am feeling injured
Turning inside out

As it sees the pain
If only I could stop it
I have come too far to see the end now
Even if my way is wrong

But I will continue
Until it stops me
There is nothing left to say
Because I will not give up

Or throw in the towel
I keep falling
In a sea of water of myself
Begging for air

Yet I still will not give up
Where do I go from here?
I asked for help
But just another pill

My tolerance I take more than prescribed
So, let the forest hear me out
Night after night
And the shadows too

May 14, 2022

Sleepy Town

This town sleeps
To become lite-up and targeted
Under watchful eyes
The powerful night enfolds all

The unbound souls are running away
Comfort found in the sanctuary
If only I could find my slumber at all
Wrapped arms around me

As morning light meets the dark
So, my heart yearns
Breaking ice shards from the wall
Like a vagrant in the cold

Looking for hope
Into a transparent world
Only to rewire the mind
Need to head in a new direction

And view my window new
Morning is meeting dark soon
And my heart is yearning too
This town sleeps

April 27, 2022

Smile In Tow

The advice is true
My heart will beat despite who I like
And stay the same if I lose
Breaking is just a metaphor

So, I look to my inner self
For answers
And hope I do not see someone else
I can feel me all the same

So, I will walk this journey
With a bright smile in tow
The night might be brighter than the light
But the light will show me what is right

March 5, 2022

So Many Faces

Out of all the faces in the crowd
Your face is all I see
It is staring at me
Beckoning beckoning

There are voices all around
But yours is all I hear
Calling to me
Only your voice comes through

As I steadfast in wait
For your footsteps to meet mine
Have I been waiting here before?
Or is it the longing

I know it is you
If you knock at my door
For I know it, is you
By the pounding of my heart

When I see so many faces
What do I see?
But traces of me
And you coming back to me

Yet I know you are not there
Forget and not care
But you are always there
So many faces and all I see is you

April 22, 2022

So, You Put it On Me

So, you put it on me
To make me feel again
Like home in the heart
Or a clear head

It is a rhyme that heats up this dance
As it beats to the rhythm
Shall I run away no more?
In this final hour

So, I feel this deep inside
Only to come alive
You hold me closer
So, I will feel the let go

Or never so
And your kisses bring me to life
How I need to be by your side
With scars and all

To feel my free complete
To rise above it all
As we lay beneath this sun
Arm and arm

Many years to come
I have but one wish
Let us not waste time
For that would be a crime

Let us look ahead
Where roses bloom
And pain flows no more
So, you put it on me

January 24, 2022

Solid Ground

I came to the ocean
To think about my life
And what lead me here
Standing on my two feet

Hiding in the shadows
Hope I have done right
And places I have never been
Is this how it all begins?

Because I am ready
I will be on my way
My heart is racing
You will see me rise

For there are mountains to climb
And with every answer, there is a new question
Is it worth all this?
I am pushing myself to the edge

I am looking for reasons
Find a shelter from the storm within
Just keep my eyes ahead
And dust me off again

May 14, 2022

Spring Changes to Fall

Spring changes to fall
But I am here to give my all
Sweet as an apple
When winter changes to spring

Or the mistletoe kiss
I will be there for these things
You make me feel invincible
Wanted and loved

My candle will not burn alone
On winters days
My days are filled with fun
On spring filled days

February 14, 2022

Stay Alive

Got a poem in my head
Must rush to get out of bed
Lights are flashing
But all I see is red

Feeling empty
But all I know is the dream I had
In a world gone shallow
In a world gone mad

Sometimes there are things a man should not know
If it is not breaking, do not fix it
Sometimes leaves do not grow
There is no place to run to

Rather focus on getting away from somewhere
I will stay with my strength tonight
Keeping it together till morning light
When I will see a new day rise

I will do what it takes to stay alive
There is a truth, and it is on my side
I have been waiting all my life
To feel my heart as it keeps time

March 23, 2022

Steady Feet

I live but it is colder now
I am just sick of it
Like I need to make a move
Shake it up a bit

There must be more to this
I am staring down at myself
Looking back at the years
Hoping to steady my ground

But every glance is killing me
Can I get redemption?
And stop the reflecting
I know I am moving

But I go nowhere
Scared is my biggest fear
But I will become what I can be
Stop the reflecting

And get to where I need to be
I will get what I deserve
Because I will work hard
Can you see what I see?

All my senses came back to me
Release the weight
Steady feet do not fail me now
I am going to run till I cannot walk

March 17, 2022

Stop the Compulsion

Stop
Working so hard
On figuring out everything
And being on yourself
The compulsion to knowing

What is next will come
Regardless of obsessive thinking

Giving too much energy
The ego will take over
And bring on the worst-case scenario

Instead, just be
Because the mind knows to do
Being comes from the soul
Trust in your soul

Obsessive thinking
Is controlling everything
Enjoy what life is

You can stay in your head
But come back to the present
And use thinking when you need it

January 24, 2022

Strangling Heart

Your heart is in pain
Even strangling
Taking your every breath
You cannot fight back

The long and lonely nights
Can anybody hear you?
Can somebody show you the light?
Is anybody there?

Surely everything will be alright
When you are not alone
You have been waiting for so long
Time waits for no one

You must carry this on your own
You may not remember how to shine
Or use your wings to fly
But someone will take your weight off

And lead you to the light
Where you will not be alone
Your heart is in pain
Even strangling

May 13, 2022

Streams Will Flow

There are no streams in these rivers that flow
Washing our hands of all the pain
Will there ever be hope in these waters?
Or bring a swimmer back to life

As we drown in the silence
Or lock away the key
It is in the easy way we talk about it
Or how we still have no children to show

But I dance again to another chance
While I feel the world go around me
I had no time to choose
What I chose to do

Just take it slow and easy
Leave room for change
Do not get stuck in ways
Or deny yourself the try

Put your best forward
And do not give up
It will get easier
Because you deserve a child

February 12, 2022

Strength Cove Me

Protect me when I hesitate
From the world that left me cold inside
In darkness be the sound and light
Take me to the other side

And all that it justifies
Then I wander away
Will this world let me find my way back?
Give me strength and heal my soul

Broken down and lost
On a path that is endless
I must go on
Time tics on

And takes no sides
Mortals burdened
Lost and blind
Taking dreams one by one

That rage upon open seas
And sirens call to lure you to your death
Only to hang from killers' trees
Follow my shadow to find me

Be the path that brings me home
When the world has failed me
I must go on
Let your strength cover me

May 9, 2022

String of Theory

String of theory holding up our race
In this astral plane in reverse
As we fall through the universe again
Among the milky ways

And down dead man's visions
Only to fade away in nuclear fission
Or dreams of fusion
Are we still holding up in this race?

Like puppets on string of theory
To feel love or life
As we fly endlessly
In the lost and found

In the universe of sinking ships
No faster than the speed of light
String of theory burns bright
Only to turn black hole sight

Fear hides the human race
Answering string of theory buried underground
To find the race endlessly in space
Will our ship be found?

As the race for human ground
Or bombs touch down
Show the puppet string theory light
As the crash hits into the night

January 13, 2022

Strong Love

I was able to fall in love with you so strong
Like nothing else was wrong
Gravity makes sense now when you are around
Because my feet have left the ground

My head is in cloud nine
Looking for reasons to shine
Deep under demons' load
Slipping to wonders of your mode

I just want to see all
So, will you give me tonight to fall?
And the rest of my life?
So, when I open my eyes to know no strife

I will be by your side
Forever happy never to hide
I was able to fall in love with you so strong
Like nothing else was wrong

February 27, 2022

Strongholds

There are better days in the end
Being strong will be your friend
Hold the fight to keep it together
It is not over you can tether

You will always have hope
To keep you on the rope
So, do not let go
For the fight will let you know

It is how you move closer to another
Putting one foot in front of the other
Pushing through this with delight
Getting through the darkness to the light

Heavy is the heart each night
Fighting the fight with light
You never know just what tomorrow holds
And you are stronger than any strongholds

March 26, 2022

Struggle to Put it Out

Caught up in this broken thing
Had a song to sing
But I cannot sing
As I struggle on the ground

Lost in the line we crossed
Had a voice to talk
But I cannot talk
As I struggle to put back the pieces

But there is a scream inside
So tight that cannot hide
Alive and will not be denied
I will put my voice out there

Find myself in melodies
To be for love
To be for life
I will shout it out like I need to do

February 19, 2022

Stuck With You

Exposed
Our love's
My skin
Stuck
Fractals
Nowhere to be found
But everywhere
Untouched
Healing
I am stuck with you

May 11, 2022

Surrender Or Update

The coldness of a room
I left behind
Means nothing at all
Lines were crossed

As you destroyed my boundaries
From where I cannot return
And my faith tried to betray me
But it led me home

Did I surrender or upgrade?
My happiness is all I must give
No questions asked just to take me in
Dismantle the ugliness that surrounds me

It has been a long time since I have been this happy
I am not too far gone
Now I can be the best that I can be
I am on my knees

I surrender to thee
Understanding more every day
Friendship, family, and emotional connections
Knowing I will be caught if I fall

And apricating the little things in life
Learning to worry less about what I cannot change
Focus on solutions and not the problem
I may miss you, but I have your memories

So, I left the cold room
Behind me now
And I surrendered
Or did I upgrade

March 27, 2022

Take Care of You

Sometimes you are alone
But you are home
It is not just how we planned it
We sure have made it work

I am happy they are throwing stones
We will build a house
And I know that you
Need someone to make it through

On days like this, I needed you too
So, I will take care of you
You will take care of me, too
If you ever feel down know I am around

March 8, 2022

Take My Life

Take my life
Or tell me where I stand
A mind unmade
How I love that no one knows

Secrets we have so far
As demons lie in the dark
Playing pretend that never ends
And no one must know

Could my cracked smile slow downtime?
If only I could call you mine
Wishing on that shooting star
So, if I stop this beating heart

Would you give me the time of day?
And say a word or two
Due to just me and you
So, take my life

March 23, 2022

Taking Pieces

Home is where the heart is
But I have not been there in a while
The same it shall stay
Just like family in that stain

How many years must I carry this blame?
Till someone takes some of the pieces off my brain
Father how I deserved your name
I am a kid with so much ambition

I came from this world
I had no idea what to become
As words spilled out, I became a king
A forgotten one but a chosen son

Cities may bury and defeat me
But I will rise along with the names of the streets
And be able to say goodbye to it all
Because I will not stay in my falls

Each day that ends it will begin again
Because innocence is gone
When satisfaction is met
Or catastrophe spilled over

Once on a journey to nowhere bound
My inhibition finally found
I am a slave to my earthly ways
Rise from my grave to find my soul

January 18, 2022

Tear Away

What you obsess over
In life
Cling to your desires
That is unattainable

Life will find away
To take
And tear them away
From your universe

February 15, 2022

That Day

My mind traps me
Not letting me erase
That moment
As it flashes back

To that day
My lips are getting looser
I do not know
What I am saying

Or what to say
As the feelings take over
My heart and mind
No one is better than anyone here

But this love for you
It is more than that
Ravages an emotion
I am face to face with myself

Because I stole my power from the sun
Yet I am weak in my thoughts
Moving on is exhausting
Trapped on that one day

March 15, 2022

The Man Below the Surface

When words are spoken
They hold presence
I feel the nervousness
As I stand with you

This is what stage fright feels like
As everyone's aura fills the room
But it is this moment in time
To be present and subline

And my thoughts echo off these four walls
Do they understand?
How many times I have practiced this before?
While they look at me

Chances given only to take a few
And countless kisses I have viewed
But tomorrow my eyes will get what is dew
As I whisper to my husband, I love you

And I belong to you
I will wait to hear his vows too
As a tear rolls down your face
Alter hear my honesty

I refuse to grow older
Unless it is with you
As I fall in love
Making promises as promises made

There are more behind these words that we have spoken
Yes, they can see us
But only briefly
Only you know the man below the surface

March 25, 2022

These Four Walls

As I stare at these four walls
My wants become my needs
I remember another time
How it felt to hold you

My head begins to spin
I still have your things
Staring at it all
Wishing we had fought harder

It is hard to move on
When we made such a mess of things
Left with failure
Broken promises

Now I can barely breath
I remember another time
My wants become my needs
As these four walls close in on me

March 30, 2022

Thoughts of You

One thought of you
Is suicide
As you linger
In the back of my mind

You will never fix this
My emotions
Will get the best of me
Giving my life for you

Like I am your savior
What a mistake
I will not be your savior
One too many lies

Now the letter is written
Read you shall not
But the lies took my love
Move on I must

March 11, 2022

Time In the Silence

I take up time in the silence
For my mind to run in circles
With my ear planted to the ground
Searching for that anecdote untold

Keeps me great when we are face to face
Sharing smiles all the while
But could you turn and be bile
Two faces of the same person

Living in misery
I will spare you sympathy
Enemy, I need you not
For I will take up time in the silence

March 27, 2022

Time My Foe

As you become my foe time
I bitterly walked through you
Cracking light underneath my skin
Or covered spots of falling hair

Yet I hear I got it wrong
In a moment somehow got it
In your strict design
My moment is your time

How could I have gotten it wrong?
I need to feel relief
Because you are bold
And believe you are here to hold

January 29, 2022

To Be Brave

Veins pumping
Faster and faster
Adrenaline rises
So, too does the promises

How to be brave?
Or to love
When I fear the fall
But you stand alone

In your doubt
Getting closer
Step by step somehow
But I die waiting for you

As time stands still
So, does your beauty
But I will be brave
Veins pumping faster and faster

January 24, 2022

To Be with You

The days are lost
The clock always said 12 o'clock
Never feeling so alive
Cannot back down now

I have lost so much time
To be with you
Nothing more to do
Nothing more to lose

To be with you
And people knew
That is why it is me and you
Here my eyes will stay

Nothing more to say
It is coming out right
All throughout the night
Head spinning with delight

In a room we made bright
Nothing to prove
Everything knew I was
To be with you

January 22, 2022

To Happen

Feeling a shift
Highly intuitive
In this hermit mode
It is a peek a boo show

Call upon thee
Only to select a few
Dare I share my visions
Gifts and peek a boos

But something big is happening

January 8, 2022

To Hold You

Now your head may rest, my love
All is going to be right
The darkness is gone
The light will shine on you

I am here
I will hold you tight
Rest now, your heart
You will be in my dreams

Nothing will make you gone
You will be alright
Although you are gone
I will be here to hold you

I have got you
I will breathe for you
And calm the storms
And keep the fires at bay

I will face down the world for you
I am here
To hold you
And calm the storms

March 5, 2022

To Live My Life

No matter how many times I wanted to live my life
No matter how many times I tried to breathe
No matter how many nights I spent alone
Where do I go

Down the rabbit hole
As days go by, the nights on fire
It is a thought a word is born
To kill a wrong and prove a right

Crushing spirits to expose the truth
You must destroy to create
This hurricane is chasing you to the underground
Until death makes you forget

But in life have no regrets
As my fire beats throughout my heart
The war rages on to riot an explosive flame
Till there is nothing left but empty space

And praying to God
Is it me you seek?
In rapture or torture, me
No matter how many times I wanted to live my life

March 24, 2022

To Say Goodbye

I had it all thought out what to say
Now as my mouth tries to move
Words escape me and the facts
This is to say goodbye

As my eyes tell lies to me
Another spell of willful compromise
I need understanding
Not another manipulation

Or a memory I will not share
Another memory I will forget
As I walk away from here
You know I am not unkind

The future is the future
The past is the past
No reason to go back
No change of heart

February 19, 2022

To the River

Take your sleeplessness to the river
Where time watches your every move
Focus your eyes on the bevers dam
Because your body is damaged

Send my regards to hell
As you fall to your knees
This to your soul they will see
So, crawl, beg, and plead

You have lost power over your destiny
Stay in the deep end
You may get a wish
Before you say goodbye

To everyone you know and love
Your pulse races with fear
As the surface reflects your skin
Your heart beats in your mouth

So, fall to your knees
Beg and plead
You lost your power
And stay here in the river

March 29, 2022

Tonight

Blue face and pale lips
Breathing cold snowflakes
On a sour tongue to ignite the lungs
Now the day brings the worst of life

Long nights and things that bite
Struggling to stay away from the stranger in the dark
Or the shadows that hide
Pulling me into a dream

Slowly sinking, wasting
Crumbling under the weight of life
And then I hear the screams or is that a siren
The worst things in life come free

Because I am under someone's thumb
Do a song and dance for a slice of bread
Will the puppet-master be kind tonight?
Or will he be on the pipe to the motherland?

And sell me out to another man
It is too cold to be a ho
For this angel will fly
With ripped gloves and two overcoats

Tring to navigate this ocean of blues
Staying afloat with wet clothes and dry news
Loose change and weary eyes
Dry throat and burnt lungs

March 25, 2022

Took My Soul

He took my soul
To the carnage of me
In my bones
I was left

To find the love you gave
Spirit flies closer
Yet I was too close to the ground
Taking my heart

Taking my soul
Leaving my carnage on this earth
As each day cuts my breath
He took my soul

January 15, 2022

Truly Love Me

Your calls just go unanswered
You think of me mean, but
You want it this way
Plus, I can treat people as objects

Changing my mind day to day
I did not mean to try you out
But I still know your birthday
So, I am sorry before I break your heart

Sorry that I cannot believe
And that nobody ever did
Want to fall in love with me
So, sorry before I break your heart

Sorry I could be so blind
I did not mean to leave you so cold
And all the things we had
You were kind and good

But you had to make it wrong
So, I understood
The way you laid your eyes on me
In ways that no one ever could

And so, it seems I broke your heart
Because now you do not understand
You fail to see what is going on
So, I tore you open till the end

I am sorry for breaking your heart
Sorry that I cannot believe
That nobody will ever
Truly fall in love with me

May 10, 2022

Truth Into Strength

Things in life can be hard
But given obstacles makes you strong
There is no perfect way to handle life
To tell you anything you need

Time will travel by the same
For everyone no matter who you are
It will turn truth into strength
Just see yourself the way I see you

I, feel it just feel it too
It will make a believer in you
Because I am a believer
Time is passing

It waits for no one
All this will turn truth into strength
But we all will be ageless
And see the light

May 11, 2022

Tucked Away in My Dreams

Sitting in my longing
Waiting for my second chance
If only something would break
Cut these chains that bind

To feel not good enough
To feel like I can
Distract the world around me
What a beautiful release

So, the memories fly away
Leaving me empty
Weightless in bondage
Maybe I will find some peace tonight

Tucked away in my dreams
Fly away from here
From this dark cold bedroom
And the perpetuity that I feel

I will be pulled from the wreckage
Sweet silence covers me
Tucked away in my dreams
Finding relief here

Walking the tight rope is not for me
And everywhere I turn
There is someone harming me
The hurricane keeps twisting

But I keep building up my armor
That I make up for all that you lack
It does not make a difference
I will just escape one last time

Because it is easier to believe
In this sweet madness
This trivial sadness
That brings me to my knees

Tucked away in my dreams
Fly away from here
From this dark cold bedroom
And the perpetuity that I feel

I will be pulled from the wreckage
Sweet silence covers me
Tucked away in my dreams
Finding relief here

March 29, 2022

Two Worlds Crashed

Perplexed
In the truth
But I will tell you
I love your soft heart

While I stand
You were too
Our two worlds crashed
We were inseparable

We could live
For a thousand years
And I will love you
For all those years

I told you
That we could fly
Because we all have wings
But some of us do not know why

Standing
You were there
Our two worlds crashed
We were inseparable

May 14, 2022

Unable

Your senses are out of reach
Even after breaking down the walls
Scratching clawing to get to you
You are untouchable

Unreachable
As you find more walls to put up
It keeps you impenetrable
Unstimulatable

Keeps you unattackable
Uncaptavatable
It will leave you unshockable
Petrifiable

Keep you undesirable
Scratching clawing to get to you
Even after breaking down the walls
Your senses are out of reach

January 19, 2022

Under This Hemisphere

I have been crawling
On my hands and knees
Begging the riverbeds
For salt to sting my wounds

I need this no
So, I let go
Under this hemisphere
To be my only way

When the storm rages on
The happiness covers the surface
Will, you not save me?
Or watch the dagger inter me

At times I live apart
Why sleep the sun has an eye on me
Staring me down
We fight again like paper Mache

Tumble and collide
Deep dark into the night
It is the only way I know
Somebody better save me

May 5, 2022

Understand It All

The wilderness works its way inside
To make the heart cold
Do you think my mind drifts when hot?
Or suddenly you have always known

But it was me all along
And I will reach the light
And understand it all
Try hard to fight

When all I want to do is fall
Into the night
Into your arms, surrender
Delay me in my rights

For you were giving me a fight
If I said I did not miss you
I lied
Told me I let you go

Into the night
Into your arms
Surrender
Maybe then I would understand it all

March 7, 2022

Unsteady

Holding myself down
Till I find my steady
My leg will not stop the move
Because I am a little unsteady

Call it excited
Approaching the near
Or am I the alone
Because it feels like I am home

Or should I let go
How the side effects affect me
But I hold on
To the steady

Or is the steady holding on to me
Because I am a little unsteady
Till I find myself steady
Holding myself down

March 2, 2022

Up Down

No backing up
Or backing down
I am on my way up
I got this role down

It is planned up
So, it will not come crashing down
Follow this sound up
And push the demons down

Take to the fire up
So, no jumping down
Keep the spirit up
And the afraid down

It is time to stand up
No time to sit down
Proud with hands up
To keep the storm down

No matter how torn up
I will not stay down
I will keep living it up
Nothing will bring me down

My cage will tear up
I will break it down
I am standing up
Facing my demons down

I am starting up
Holding my ground down
I am so fed up
Had enough of going down

Put my life back up
No more looking down
My direction is up
I am proud not down

January 13, 2022

Violent Stare

Never should have picked up the phone
I heard your voice you were the one
Only to build me up and tear me down
Like you do all the rest

It is in your eyes when you left
Just left me cold and out of breath
I admit I feel too hard
Just went into you too deep

I knew cruelty existed
I should have started running
A long time ago
But I never thought you would

Be the one to run this into the ground
So, I am getting closure
As I get better and better
Picking up the pieces

Gluing my heart back together
Wishing I never met you
And that violent stare
Like a hammer to my heart

Dragging memories to a fade
Packed bags in a hallway
Because there is nothing left to say
As the door slams shut

Another one opens
Getting over you
Moving on to brighter days
Leaving your violent stare

February 11, 2022

Walked Out

Walked out of your bedroom
With words, I traded you
Laid your head at the foot of the bed
You wept

Playing it back in the other room
Breaking up like I always do
I know you love me
I love you too

Causing a lonely heart
Now lost in the wilderness
In the dark, we are fighting in it
I did not mean to leave you like this

I can hold you tight
Fake forgiveness and take a bow
I will love you still
I know your heart will still be lonely

This is the hardest part
Wasting your heart for my heart
It is you that needs me
But I walked out of the bedroom

May 4, 2022

Want To Play

You think you want to play
It is a fool's choice
I am the player of players
I am the king of sorrow

To beat me you must lose
I will spear your soul if you sell me your life
Look into my eyes
See how many demons come to your rescue

Or will my mind find you first
Only a lover knows what your life is worth
If the demons do not get to you first
Hold on to your Godhead

For the devil will look for your weakness
I am the player of players
It is a fool's choice
You think you want to play

March 24, 2022

Watch That Spot

Hello
I know you can hear me
I call you every day
To tell you I love you

It is lunchtime
You are happy today
You must be busy at work
That is great I will be home soon

And I will have a surprise
Everything will be wonderful
You sound great
I love you

If you ever miss me
Go outside
Look up at the sky
Know I am looking at the same spot

Whenever you need me
That spot will be ours
Whenever I am gone too long
If your lips, feel lonely

That spot is ours
But you will never have to wait long
Keep in mind
We are under the same sky

With clouds of many
To call upon you
If you feel
You cannot wait

Look upon that spot
Because I will watch it too
I know you can hear me
I call you every day

May 14, 2022

We Succeeded

Some days you may be close to the ground
Even inside out
Feeling like you're falling apart
And someone broke your heart

But this will not hold you down
Not while I am around
You are stronger than you think
You will be happy again

Happiness is a choice
I hope you get what you wish for
And you're well understood
As I look at you

You have a lot to be thankful for
Beauty and a family too
And me standing here
Holding your hand so tight

Each and every night
Till you are not falling
Inside out
Falling apart

Or feeling a broken heart
I was there to get you out of bed
To make it through another day
Because you will be happy

I hope you get what you wish for
And you're well understood
The process works, and you worked it
Now the world is yours to take

Breathe in your opportunities and go
I will always be with you
Do not forget what happened
And how we succeeded

March 28, 2022

Welcome Mat

My welcome mat
It is more than just an invitation
In the sun
Or by the light of the moon

Come inside
I am home
Or I will be soon
The numbers hang above my door

Listening and waiting for you adore
To stand inside and bring joy
One by one
Or two by two

It is not far to go
Once you pass the welcome mat
I will give my all
Just to see you

And reach you
So, come inside
It is more than just an invitation
My welcome mat

January 29, 2022

Went Over the Fence

As you went over the fence
To taller and greener grass
Let me tell you it will not last
My mind knows this hell to well

It will rip a hole in us
Stripping away our heart
But you think you need more
An ache to fill like something new

That man is looking good to you
Grass is greener
On the other side of the fence
Believe that it is even taller

Nothing wrong with that
But I would have taken a bullet for you
Even walked through fire
My vows for you were true

But you blew it, and you knew
Getting old is not to be feared
No demons here
But you broke your promises

Now you are gone
The locks are changed
Your clothes are packed
You went over the fence

January 26, 2022

With Your Smile

You never wanted to walk alone
And hated being on your own
We always walked hand and hand
You need me the words I heard all too well

Doing everything in love that was right
Praying what lay upon your eyes was real
And the words believe me comes out of your mouth
As day follows the midnight sky

Could you be lost for words?
In a pool of emotions
Then a thought was lost in our space
Because you killed me with your smile

Beautiful, wild, and soft
It is that smile that keeps me here
Keeping me thinking of that first kiss
As the hands would turn with time

You would always say you were mine
Turning and lending a smile
To whisper it is a new night
And danced into my life

Like a symphony
Like a lover's song
Yes, you killed me with your smile
Through the darkest night

And the brightest light
You are the light that shines
Deep inside
It is who you are

March 24, 2022

Without You

Words spoke to spoil the mode
The carnage left in your wake
How you turned from Jekyll to Hyde
To build me up and tear me down

Like I meant nothing at all
Even spared nothing when you left
Just left me cold and out of breath
Did you have to say forever?

Did I have to fall so deep?
Guess I let you get the best of me
I did not see it coming
The flags were there

I should have gone running
But I took a risk
Left no room for doubt
But I will be better off without you

Now that I am getting closure
The pieces will fit back together
Better than you know
Now that I am without you

March 26, 2022

Worn Bones

To a day's end
Bones wore down
It was in the know this would get rough
So, let me see what happens

I cannot get enough
I know this love is pain
But it will cut us every time
If we lock the doors

Leave the lights on in the room
Do not walk away
This pain will hurt tonight
To a day's end and worn bones

February 14, 2022

Wounds Will Heal

As I sit in the here and now
I get so tired of being here
Because I am locked in this fear
Childish as they may be

If you leave, then leave
Your presence feels like you are gone
How these scars left wounds
And the pain is just too real

The lies were too many to keep up with
Time cannot erase
Did I mean anything to you?
Or the tears I wiped away?

I even fought the demons you feared
And I held your hand through all these years
I will still have me to keep me sane
Even after all this, all this is gone away

Bound to the life you left me behind
To face the haunted dreams
That comes my way
But these wounds will heal another day

March 3, 2022

Woven Thoughts

Every thought is woven
Weaving through a tapestry of us
My soul is yours to take
In a moment in time, I captured you

These scars are ours to bare
In a time, looped and woven
It will clear you
And your conscience

I will be whatever you need
Share memories with myself
Just keep my thoughts
And use my wisdom

We are not selfish if we are together
You will always find yourself
Every thought still stands apart
Weaving in and out of hours and days

May 12, 2022

Years Have Passed

Years have passed since I have been here
But the streets are the same it is clear
Memories all around me
Old ones, ready to build new ones and be free

In the dead of the night, the nightmares do not start
I have a fistful of belief in myself because I am smart
I am back to where I buried that memory
I hear it calling out to me

Or is it in my head
But I am back ahead
The streets are the same
Years have passed since I have came

March 26, 2022

Yes, I am Changing

It is quite
You could hear a pin drop
I am raging
Late into the night

As demons cultivate
Throughout the world
Whispering in my ear
Wrecking my emotions

Turning me to hate
Changing me
Moving me
Yes, I am changing

March 8, 2022

You Are on the Path

On my journey
In the world unknown
Just roaming
Visions sparkle

As I get to know
In my quandary
Just rolling
Out in the open

It was a wish
Tossed a penny in a wishing well
To see a dream come true
Only time will tell

So, I roll along
A mission to see God's plan through
A feeling, that I am unstoppable
A mission not impossible

I am the gatekeeper of my mind
I have the key to unlocking all my potential
Clarity brings purpose
A peace that is bestowed in happiness

And the will to be strong mentally
The rolling is over
No more roaming
I am on the path to enlightenment

April 23, 2022

You Complete Me

Sometimes I am in the ocean
And the tide is pulling me under
It leaves me feeling incomplete
But you always tell me

Things will change
I will shine like a star
It is time that is given to the heart
I will be yours

And you will be mine
We will not worry about things we do not need
Before we both run out of time
We are going to see

That we will be all that we need
I have been the best and been the worst
Been a ghost in a crowded room
I took a chance

And it led to you
Sometimes I am in the ocean
And the tide is pulling me under
It leaves me feeling incomplete

May 14, 2022

You Opened My Heart

We were fearless
And we were in love
We were lighter than air
Nothing could bring us down

We were never coming to the ground
Close it up and be my reason
I will never leave your side
Because you are worth every bit of my life

No one else is worth my while
You opened my heart
Put me down in my darkest dark
All the while we used to laugh

We were links in a beat-up chain
Puzzle pieces on a beat-up game
But we will outlive the rest
Close it up and be my reason

March 7, 2022

You Say You Are

Could I have said it
Or got it off my chest
Only to bring anger
And malice

You are not a man
That you say you are
You cannot fill the holes
With money or words

You are not even half the man
You say you are
I am glad I never
Married you

But I should have
Never felt sorry for you
Or tried to help you
Now I am over you

February 16, 2022

You Will

Your past and pain put you here
Hitting rock bottom and full of fear
Your heart is cold, and your walls are tall
Let us re-write this story before you take a fall

You feel broken and falling apart
I am here for you so you will not lose
Even though you are lost on these lonely nights
Trying to kill the pain you are feeling

I will be here now for your healing
Trying to chase away your demons
I hear your screams within your nightmares
And how you tell me you are lost within your stares

There is darkness in this space
But you will not fall from grace
You will kill the pain inside
Mend your heart and see the light

March 26, 2022

Your Love Cost

Your love cost
I cannot even buy
True but happy
With lies

But questions why
It beats knowing you
A perfect day blues
Granting wishes on falling stars

Still, I question why
It beats knowing you
Your love cost
It is tough to know

love is kind
To carry out a wish
like mine
Heading for higher ground

March 2, 2022

Your Poem

I get that feeling
Every time you are around
It is something I just cannot hide
Ten thousand miles separate us

But we live together in our hearts
I work magic to show
And create a passion to grow
I know it is not much

But it is the best I can do
My gift to you is poems
And this one is for you
You make life worth living

And it is you that everything is giving
I work toward protecting
When you love someone
You naturally protect

March 12, 2022

Your Story Untold

I saw through you
When you get wiser you will too
I knew it all along
Your luck will be strong

But every stroke of luck must bleed through
Bleed out
Held by the balance of time
Even the blind can see through

I could read you like a book
You thought your story was untold
Your life forward and slow
Making it a race to the end

Well look at yourself now
There is no one else but you
And you are not even on the surface
You talk like you are here

No, I hear someone else though
It only revs up the nerves
You were the better part
Of how I could feel

And my beating heart
I now know the lonely heart
Blackened heart and bone flesh
Because you were somebody else

February 21, 2022